WE SHARE THE SAME SKY

WE SHARE

THE SAME SKY

A MEMOIR OF
MEMORY & MIGRATION

RACHAEL CERROTTI

**BLACK
STONE**
PUBLISHING

Printed in the United States of America

First edition: 2021

ISBN 978-1-0941-5372-8

Biography & Autobiography / Personal Memoirs

1 3 5 7 9 10 8 6 4 2

CIP data for this book is available
from the Library of Congress

Blackstone Publishing

31 Mistletoe Rd.

Ashland, OR 97520

www.BlackstonePublishing.com

For Sergiusz, for teaching me how to live with love.
For Mutti, for teaching me how to live with loss.

CONTENTS

FOREWORD

There is a part of me that wants to cry when I read this book, but then I find myself laughing. There is a part of me that wants to despair at the pity of it all, but there is just too much hope imbued in every page to give up on humanity, despite its worst excesses. That is because Rachael Cerrotti's *We Share the Same Sky* shows the tangled and messy nature of being human at its very essence.

I do wonder how a woman so young could have traveled so far, loved so deeply, listened so carefully, lived life and confronted death so profoundly that she so deftly guides us through the world's most terrifying mysteries. Circumstances placed Rachael at the fulcrum of life and death, despair and hope, past and future, allowing her an inescapably complex viewpoint of humanity and more wisdom than most acquire in a lifetime.

This book is all about the Holocaust and yet *not* about the Holocaust at all. As the granddaughter of Holocaust survivor Hana Dubová, Rachael is emblematic of what becomes of those who survive it, how memory travels across generations, how unavoidable its clutches are, and yet how to shine a light on its shadow, two generations on. Rachael tells her grandmother's story through her own words—diaries, letters, conversation, testimony— but also through the lives of those who knew her and those who saved her. And that in itself is the point: there is hope in this book, because Hana Dubová was saved by good people who took death-defying risks, because one life mattered enough.

I have observed many descendants of the Holocaust grapple with their family's past. They watch movies, read books, or sit for hours listening to their forebears recount their testimonies for USC Shoah Foundation, the archive founded by Steven Spielberg to ensure their stories would be told in their own words. Many descendants have traveled to the places of their grandparents' births or incarcerations, walking arm in arm with the survivors where they suffered as children. But I have *never* come across a descendant who has so completely lived the life of a forebear as Rachael Cerrotti lived the life of Hana Dubová. She literally retraced every footstep and went to the places of Hana's past, not for a week just to peek, but for months on end, living the life, hearing the language, learning the culture. The people who knew her grandmother's story became among her closest friends. She made her grandmother's former homes and hiding places *her* homes, *her* places to hide. Rachael's total commitment to memory was to soak up the meaning of inheritance and identity. She did what few of us rarely do: she made it her life to learn about life.

What Rachael seemed to know is that her jumbled identity was not a godforsaken hand-me-down but a tapestry of individual stitches that needed to be understood to appreciate the whole. As you read this book, you will see each of those colorful stitches painfully embroidered into her life one by one. It's only when you stand back at the end that you will see the mosaic of humanity it represents.

The backdrop to this book is big theater: World War II, the mass murder of European Jewry; one of the most daring wartime rescue missions; two thousand years of monotheistic antipathy; terrorist shootings in Copenhagen; racial tensions in America; refugees streaming over borders in the twenty-first century. The magic is in the everyday details—adapting to life on a Danish farm, finding nude photographs in old photo albums, learning language after language, and countless train, plane, and boat rides in country after country.

We relive Rachael's quest for identity, but this is not a book about her. This book is about all of us and how we confront the story of our own lives, past and present. Rachael did not choose the hand she was given, or the tragedy that unfolded in her young adulthood, but she walked the path she had not chosen with dignity and insight, and through it became a guide to life's many uncertainties.

With this book, I am left feeling more curious about my own past and present and the many people in it. *We Share the Same Sky* is about the parcel of identities that is delivered with us on the day we are born. The question is whether we have the courage and curiosity to open up that parcel and journey with its content throughout our lives, and maybe one day share its wondrous mysteries as Rachael Cerrotti has so eloquently chosen to do.

Stephen D. Smith, PhD
Finci-Viterbi Executive Director,
USC Shoah Foundation
Los Angeles, 2020

PREFACE

This is a story of memory.
But no one's memory is on trial in this book.
This is a story of history.
But the retelling of history has become the history itself.

I inherited my grandmother's love of symbolism. I was born in 1989, just a week after the first George Bush took office. That same year, the Berlin Wall fell, the Soviet Union broke apart, same-sex rights were granted in Denmark, free elections happened for the first time in Poland, and the Velvet Revolution took place in Czechoslovakia. As my life was beginning in Boston, the boundaries and borders of my ancestral continent were shifting and reshaping.

When I was twelve and becoming a bat mitzvah, as Jewish tradition expects, I was a secular preteen living in a post-9/11 world. (The Twin Towers fell just weeks before this personal milestone.) Family history had always mattered to my parents; they both held onto their roots with affection. I knew from a young age that my maternal grandparents fled during World War II and that my paternal grandparents fought in it. War was a piece of our life—not in a way that burdened us, but certainly in a way that it was given a voice. For both my mother and my father, World War II was the context of their childhoods. The history was present, even if thousands of miles away and many years ago.

Around the time of my bat mitzvah, my mom discovered that a Torah saved during the Holocaust from my grandmother's hometown of Kolín,

Czechoslovakia, had found a new home at a nearby synagogue in Massachusetts. She wrote to the rabbi and asked if I could read from it during the ceremony. He agreed. Lending us the nearly three-hundred-year-old scroll was an extreme exception, and an honored one. I knew it was special, but I was still just a young girl and unable to grasp the symbolism of chanting the words to a story that preceded me by thousands of years. My grandmother wrote me a letter a few weeks later: "Dearest Rachael, You did me and all of us proud . . . You know who you are and where you come from. Your roots are certainly deep, which you proved reading from the Kolín Torah. Maybe my father (your great-grandfather) read from it on his bar mitzvah."

Many years later, well into my deep dive into my grandmother's wartime experience, I was hired by this synagogue where the Kolín Torah lived to teach Holocaust history to their high school students; I taught them my grandmother's story. The memory of my bat mitzvah has evolved over the years. It has matured and become deeper and more textured with time.

I wrote this book throughout my twenties and into the first years of my thirties. The story I have striven to tell is ever changing. There are certain themes that I gravitated to at the start of this project—statelessness, displacement, identity—that still hold my interest, but as with my bat mitzvah, the story has grown up as I have grown up. I am sure that one day, if I become a mother or have the privilege of being a grandmother, I will have something different to say.

Every story in this book is accurate as one remembers it. I have fact-checked these memories only when a statistic like someone's age or a date did not cohere. There are cracks in all our memories; sometimes they are exposed by our own inconsistencies, sometimes they are challenged by other people's perspectives, and sometimes they change with time. The quotes in this book have been approached with the same trustfulness given to memory. Some have been stitched together or had their spelling or punctuation altered for clarity, and some have been edited for brevity. Personal names have been written in their native form; I have not anglicized people's names unless they themselves chose to do so. I have taken a similar approach to the spellings of most place-names and to words or phrases spoken in languages other than English. In short, I have translated only where it felt necessary.

I've had to ask myself a lot of questions while writing this book to figure out how I could remain truthful to the flexibility of memory. What does one do when a feeling recorded years ago no longer rings true? Does one use what it felt like then, or does one adjust the narrative to reflect the present? Which is more honest? more authentic? more useful? What happens when new facts emerge—ones that change context? Do newly uncovered details replace old feelings? The answer I have settled on for this story is to simply write what feels right.

I am writing this preface in the summer of 2020. We are living through a pandemic, and I have been quarantining in my little basement apartment in Newton, Massachusetts, for almost half a year. I was supposed to be in Europe right now with many of the people you will meet in this book. I genuinely don't know when I will ever see them again, or even if I will. It is a strange existence. I flip the pages between past and present without seeing much of a difference anymore. I don't know what the world will look like when this book will be published or in the coming years, but I do know that the evolving relevance of history is one of our few certainties.

I will conclude with two thoughts: the first is that my grandmother never had a bat mitzvah. That wasn't something girls did in her time. I imagine how different her life would have been had she grown up in a different time and place. I am certain she would have been a professional writer as well. Her words are found throughout this book, and they are beautiful.

The second thought is this: around the time my grandmother was the age of a bat mitzvah, she was trying to understand why life had become a series of muffled conversations. Her family lived in a democracy. They were secular. They were assimilated. They were protected. The hate and the persecution in Nazi Germany and the recently annexed Austria weren't fathomable in their country. Her parents repeated over and over again, "It could never happen here." How wrong they were.

Read with kindness,
Rachael Cerrotti
(Hana's granddaughter)

August 8, 1992

Dearest Rachael,

Do you miss me? I miss you terribly. It's a week since I saw you.

I miss you running into me and "goring" me with your head and then laughing with delight. What a beautiful laugh you have!! Your entire being is full of joy and delight, and your cunningness takes me by surprise. I miss seeing you eating with such a hearty appetite. As your Ima says, you eat as if you were a teenage boy.

You're sturdy in body and spirit. Full of confidence in your abilities, as you want to do everything for yourself, by yourself, yet at the same time you're social and love interaction.

You can distinguish the beautiful from the mundane. Where did you learn to comment, to give compliments on clothing?

I not only miss your smile and your laugh, but also your frown and your curiosity.

Do you remember we slept together in the cabin? Do you remember me reading the book *One Morning in Maine*, and you, knowing it by heart, kept correcting me? We read by flashlight under the sleeping bag. And when your eyes were closed, I stopped reading only to be told in a commanding tone to continue.

Yes, we all were in your parents' cottage for one week. Jesse, who was a delight, your father, your Ima, Rebecca for a few days, your Aunt Nina and your cousins Elana, Yoel, and Daniel (with whom you had several fights for possessions), Bernd, and myself. What a crowd!! It was so much fun and pleasure.

I often think how lucky I am, how lucky Ima is, how lucky you are having such a loving extended family. Your Ima didn't have the pleasure of or the luxury of having grandparents. She as well as Aunt Nina and Uncle Peter (father of your favorite cousins, Ross and Emily) had only a nuclear family.

When you're much older and I'm still around, I'll tell you about it.

The world was bad, crazy, and vengeful then. And today, half a century later, it's not better by much. People will always fight for one reason or another and kill each other.

We're in August 1992.

We had presidential elections. George Bush is president and wants to be again next term. Bill Clinton, Democrat, is running against him.

The 25th Olympic Games are taking place in Barcelona, Spain.

In Somalia, children by the hundreds are dying of hunger and illness.

Israel has a new prime minister, Rabin, who is more willing to give into Palestinian demands than his predecessor, Shamir, was.

There is a terrible civil war in Yugoslavia. Serbs are killing Croats and vice versa. Small children are killed and/or separated from their parents for no reason and no fault. They didn't do anything bad.

You are lucky to live in a country where you are protected by us all. You'll grow up to be as compassionate as your parents, who are concerned about the human race, as well as the environment (which is getting polluted).

In the cottage in Maine, which is a beautiful state, we forget about it all. The outside world. Didn't even listen to the radio.

We just enjoyed each other, and mainly, I enjoyed so much spending this precious week with you.

I am so grateful for it.

I am only sorry that you live so far away and I cannot see you more often.

Hope to see you soon.

With all my love,

Mutti.

Before I start writing my "new journal," I want to look back into the past. In fact, I am in the past and remember the past, but I want to keep it for the future.

—HANA'S DIARY, JULY 14, 1940

CHAPTER 1

MUTTI

Rachael, the biggest difference between your travels and mine is that I had to burn all of my bridges as I moved forward.

—HANA DUBOVÁ, 2010

I don't cry when I meet the dead. I learned this when my grandmother passed away. I was twenty-one years old and a senior in college when my aunt gently woke me to tell me that Mutti was gone.

I don't remember driving to Mutti's apartment, but I do remember standing next to her bed. She looked so small and frail, content even, as if at peace with the notion that her time had come. It was as if she had been waiting. She had talked about it so much in the previous weeks and years, aching for the answer to the question, What have I left for the world?

As a young teenager, I remember her wishes for death being emotionally violent. From the top of the staircase in the vacation house my father had built in Maine, I remember listening, as if it were a forbidden activity, while my parents tried to calm my grandmother as she demanded to be left for dead. The three-day-long Monopoly game my younger brother and I were playing would be temporarily abandoned when these episodes began.

Outside, the leaves stood still. Inside, Mutti's words reverberated off the wooden walls I had watched my dad paint with precision. There hadn't even been time for the paint to chip before Mutti's breakdowns began.

This wasn't the grandmother I knew. The grandmother I knew was filled with joy. The grandmother I knew would be asking us to play Scrabble and chasing us around the house with her pointer finger, our socks slipping on the floor as we laughed with fright knowing that once she caught us, she would tickle us until we cried. The grandmother I knew would be reading a book, walking in the woods, or swimming in Knights Pond. The grandmother I knew wanted to be here. She loved life.

At the top of the stairs I sat silently feeling numb, sliding my wool socks from one side of the steps to the other. I became a good observer this way, simply soaking in the experiences I witnessed but did not understand. It was here, in the most serene place I know, where I first remember meeting my grandmother's grief. It was my first experience seeing what inner demons run toward us when we stand still for too long.

Mutti's name was Hana Dagmar Dubová, but everyone in the family called her Mutti. It means "mother" in German. In America, my grandmother spelled her name as Hanna or Hannah and in Prague, as a child, she was fondly referred to as Hanka or Haja. She was the matriarch of our family. She swam regularly and played bridge with friends. She went to book clubs and museums. She took history tours and wore a pin that declared her an "outrageous older woman." Sometimes at holiday dinners, she would slam her fist on the table and state, "I demand respect," when she wanted to speak. Then, at the end of those dinners, she would let us grandchildren make her these disgusting concoctions of turkey fat, milk, hot sauce, orange juice, and the juice of herring. Literally anything edible was considered a possible ingredient. When we kids presented her with the specialty drink, she'd chug the whole thing and then hand the glass back. She would do anything to make us laugh.

As a grandmother, she was wild, and all of my friends (who also called her Mutti) knew this to be true. She was the crazy lady who ate fire, dyed her hair green for my bat mitzvah, and who came to my cousin's frat house to hang out with us college kids. I even smoked pot with her once.

The walls of her apartment were covered with paintings of Prague and masks from her world travels. Tables displayed paperweights and framed pictures. There were photos of us grandchildren and of the family she had lost in the war. In her home, the division between what happened in her life prior to being a refugee and what she made of her life after was minimal. It was all swept up into one long adventure. Her story surrounded us in a matter-of-fact way. It was the fabric of our family, the tablecloth used for every meal. Mutti was a Holocaust survivor—it was why our parents had no grandparents and why we had each other.

I didn't grow up living close to Mutti. My mom, Janet, was the child who moved away—from Philadelphia to Boston. She was a twenty-eight-year-old social worker when she met my dad in the basement of a liberal Protestant church. He was the reverend, and she worked for an organization that rented the space. They would sometimes meet at the water fountain outside her office and talk about philosophy and religion. They were both middle children from immigrant families, and hippies. My dad was the type of hippie who was a conscientious objector from the Vietnam War and marched in the streets. My mom, who was ten years younger, wore flowing skirts while sitting in the grass with friends who strummed the guitar. They married in 1986, and I was born in 1989.

I was raised Jewish, but for a brief period I would also go to church on Sundays to hear my father preach. That was after he had formally converted to Judaism. A modest church he had once worked for that had a dwindling congregation asked him to be their minister again as they closed down. For the most part, I didn't think about the fact that I was Jewish very often. It was kind of a moot point. Occasionally I would get the question, "But your last name is Cerrotti. You're Italian. How can you also be Jewish?" I remember trying to be cool by saying my dad had converted but that he still had family in the Italian Mafia (a lie), as if this would earn me redemption points. I didn't think my friends expected me to be ashamed of being Jewish, but I definitely didn't get the impression that I should embrace it.

Judaism only really became a point of recognition when I would visit Mutti and the rest of the family. We all ranged in our degrees of religiosity. My mom raised me and my brother reform, her brother raised his family conservative, and her sister kept an orthodox household. I found the whole thing more curious than complicated. I remember at a cousin's bar mitzvah, which was at an orthodox synagogue, observing the women confined to a sliver of the room. We had to peer through small openings in order to watch the ceremony. Mutti, ever the audacious one, pushed aside one of the curtains so she could see her grandson. The men, horrified by what she did, pulled it back. So, Mutti once again pushed it aside.

Going to see my grandmother felt like being a tourist. Since my family lived in Boston and the rest of my mom's family lived near Philadelphia, it was our responsibility to visit them. The trips always began in Boston's Back Bay Station. I remember pulling my own luggage as my mom, younger brother Jesse, and myself made our way to the Amtrak waiting area. (My dad usually stayed home.) On the train, I would sit next to a series of strangers, entertaining myself with some sort of word-search activity while my mom and Jesse sat across the aisle. Quietly, for six hours, I would watch as we passed from state to state, from Rhode Island to Connecticut to New York. We disembarked at Philadelphia's 30th Street Station, where Mutti would pick us up and drive us to her home in the suburbs. It always felt like a special occasion when we came to town.

As all of us cousins grew older, out of childhood and into our teens and young adulthood, I realized how different my relationship was with my grandmother than the family who had grown up near her. It felt like a responsibility to get to know her, a fleeting opportunity that I had missed with my other grandparents. So when I went to college, I moved close to her. And when I couldn't stand college anymore and began to wander the world, we became close.

It was a little over a year before she passed away that I asked Mutti to tell me her story. My request was twofold. First, I wanted to spend one-on-one time with her and figured this was a good way to do that. I understood that she wouldn't be around forever. Second, and perhaps somewhat selfishly, I thought it would be of value to me in the future to have her testimony—a grandmother's legacy to her granddaughter.

I made the request when we were sunbathing by her apartment complex's pool. Her wrinkles were as deep then as my skin was smooth. I was twenty years old and going into my junior year of university. I was struggling with college culture and had recently taken time off from school, beginning a pattern of moving from one place to another—Israel, Boston, rural California—sustaining myself by working in restaurants and bars. I was set to leave the country again a few weeks later to spend the year studying in Jerusalem at Hebrew University's Rothberg International School.

"Mutti, will you tell me your story?" I asked her that day. My face was shaded by an umbrella, while the rest of my body lay soaking up the sun. Nina—my mom's older sister—was with us, swimming her daily laps. Every so often she would stop to spray Sun In into my hair, determined to turn me blond.

"Why?" Mutti asked.

I shrugged. "Because I want to write it down."

I had heard her story many times, at least pieces of it. My grandmother was a regular speaker at schools, synagogues, and Holocaust commemoration events. She had visited my classrooms before. But as much as I thought I knew about her past and was aware that she had already recorded it, something inside me said the story would be different if we documented it together.

So on that afternoon in August 2009, my grandmother and I had our first storytelling session. We sat on her balcony, overlooking the generic parking lot adjacent to her building in the suburbs of Philadelphia. She talked and I wrote. In front of us were a couple of small glasses of expired boxed wine I had found in her kitchen, some small houseplants, and a pack of cigarettes she secretly smoked. My computer sat atop my bare legs, freshly pink from the morning sun.

"My mother came out of five children and one son. There were six of them," she began. "The son was the youngest. When I was a young girl, my grandfather said that after the son was born, they 'closed the shop.' But I could never understand what he meant because his store was always open.

"My mother was very much in love with my father, but during that time, siblings had to get married in chronological order. They married off Ella, my mother's older sister, and made a *shidduch*, an arranged marriage. Today they do that on computers. They matched her up. A year later my mother married my father. She was nineteen and he was twenty-six. I was born on her twentieth birthday at home."

"Do you think it is better when people get married younger?" I asked.

"I think about this often," she said. "But at that time, women were housewives or helped their husbands; they didn't have their own careers. It was a given that women ruled the household and men brought the money home. The division of labor was good at the time. It worked. I don't know how many problems they had or how happy or unhappy they were."

Hana was born on July 2, 1925 in Kolín, a small town not far from Prague, just seven years after the birth of Czechoslovakia. When she was a year old, her parents, Emilie and Josef Dub (Dubová is the female form of the name in Czech), moved the family to Prague, where they made a comfortable life for themselves. Josef owned a children's clothing store in the Old Town Square, and they lived as members of a society that valued the dreamers and the artists as much as the academics and the engineers.

"I had a brother who was four years younger than I, and when I found out that I was going to have a sibling, I still believed a stork brought the children. So every night I put poppy seeds on the balcony to feed the stork to ensure a healthy baby.

"My brother's name was Petr, and he was born in 1929. I loved, loved, loved him dearly. I really was a protective big sister. He was extremely brilliant. He could have been something. His birthday was June 30. My mother's birthday was July 1, and I was born July 2; so every time my mother was mad at us, she would say that we were the worst birthday presents; and then when her birthday came around, we were the best."

Hana, Petr, Josef, and Emilie all slept in one bedroom in an apartment that had a kitchen and dining room but no running water, bathroom, or toilet. There was a wraparound balcony that connected all of the apartments, and at the end of this were two toilets that could be accessed with keys. "There was no toilet paper. It didn't exist," she told me. "So every Sunday we would have a job to cut the newspaper into rectangles. We hung the pieces on a nail and used it as toilet paper. This is why Nina says that I lived with the dinosaurs. It was fun to cut the newspaper. Sometimes you would cut the funnies, and then when you sat on the toilet, you could read them."

Stories like these made it easy to listen to my grandmother. I knew we were embarking on a war story, but she made it sound as though we were preparing for an around-the-world adventure. She lingered on seemingly insignificant details, painting for me a picture of a place I didn't know, particularly the memories of visiting her grandparents:

"My father's family was very poor. My grandparents sold charcoal, coal, and wood for heating. Sometimes when the mountain of black soot was high, Petr and I would sit on potato sacks and slide down it, creating an avalanche behind us. And my uncle sold ice cream from a pushcart. He had vanilla, strawberry, and sometimes chocolate ice cream and sold them from these big buckets. When he was sold out, Petr and I could go and lick the rest of the ice cream out of the buckets. But the fear we had was their geese. We had to pass by them to go to the outhouse. The geese were hissing and hissing, and I was really petrified of them, so I always waited as long as I could before going to the outhouse."

One of Hana's proudest moments was when she was first allowed to take the train by herself to Kolín to visit her grandparents. As the train moved, the countryside became her own private impressionist painting as the light through the windows illuminated otherwise ordinary images. It made her feel so grown up to take these trips, as if she could handle anything. Later she was often tasked with supervising her brother on the train, guiding him through the corridors as he, too, observed a world of his own making.

Hana's maternal grandparents, the Fiala family, were far wealthier than her paternal grandparents, which was rare in a culture of dowries. They had a nice home with a beautiful garden. In the middle stood a great old oak tree, and there were flowerbeds bordered by upside-down green bottles, their necks buried in the ground. Hana, Petr, and their cousins invented all sorts of games to play in the gazebo when they weren't tasked with chores.

Hana loved to visit the general store her grandparents owned on the main square. It was called *Fialkovy Dum*, or "The House of Little Violet." They sold all kinds of garden tools, bolts of colorful fabric, knitting needles of different sizes, wool in various colors, hair clips, ornamental ladies' combs, and elastics as well as needles and canvases for needlepoint. Hana loved to explore the five shallow drawers under the counter, where hundreds of inexpensive glass rings were kept. She would slide them onto her fingers, admiring how they glittered in the light. One day she took two of them.

"I was convinced that the dog saw me and that I'd be punished for that, but the temptation was too big," she confessed. "I took the rings and hid them in my shoes. The sad part was that I had no one to show them to."

For two nights she prayed not to be punished for her sin and on the third day begged her grandmother to let her go to the store, where she slipped the rings back into the drawer.

Hana attended a German-speaking public elementary school where the students were expected to keep their hands behind their backs to encourage good posture. They had to memorize multiplication tables and long poems by Goethe, Schiller, and other famous German poets. They were expected to know the dates of major European wars and learned about faraway places such as California. Hana strove to be the best student in class, knowing that she would be allowed to walk the teacher's dog as a reward.

In fourth grade, Hana's parents transferred her to a Czech-speaking public school. By this time, Adolf Hitler had consolidated his power in Germany. That happened in 1933, six months after he became chancellor. In just half a year, he turned a democracy into a one-party dictatorship. He drafted emergency legislation that suspended civil liberties. He got rid of habeas corpus, deputized the storm troopers, and targeted communists, socialists, state delegates, homosexuals, Jehovah's Witnesses, the mentally disabled, Germans of African descent, and Jews. He overfilled the jails and then used schools and gymnasiums to hold his prisoners. And when those were over capacity, he built concentration camps. He murdered his opponents and burned their books. He amended the German constitution and gave himself emergency powers. But all this notwithstanding, the mantra in Hana's world was steadfast: "It could never happen here. Not in our young country. This will never, never happen in our democratic Czechoslovakia."

The Czech Jews were assimilated; they lived in a country that was established on the foundation that all national minorities were to be protected—Jews included. Each of the previous generations in her family had faced anti-Semitic rhetoric, sometimes being called "dirty Jews" or being spat at, but it never went any further, at least not in Hana's memory.

She was simply taught to not make waves about her Judaism—to not fight back—and for the most part, she never felt like she had to.

She told me, "On my birth certificate, it has my mother's name, my father's name, my father's profession, as well as my religion. But it doesn't say 'Jewish'; it says I was an 'Israelite.' And remember, this was prior to the state of Israel. So all 'Israelites' paid the Jew tax. I think the whole setup was pretty good. Some of the money collected went to the upkeep of the synagogue."

They didn't keep kosher, and neither did her grandparents. And no one spoke Yiddish. They attended synagogue for major holidays and family events. "We were not 'synagogue-goers,' so to speak. We didn't observe Shabbat or anything like that. Today you would call us High Holiday Jews."

Hana's Jewish identity was most connected to her involvement with the Zionist youth movement, which she joined as a preteen. Zionism, as a movement dedicated to establishing a nation for the Jewish people, was established in the late 1880s, only a couple of years after the term *anti-Semitism* was officially coined. The specific program that Hana was involved with—Hashomer Hatzair—was founded in 1913, just a few years before the First World War. The youth program was a way for Hana and her peers to be Jewish without focusing on religion. They engaged in sports programs, went to summer camps, and learned outdoor skills. The group of youngsters were called *chalutzim* (pioneers), and they dreamed of creating a Jewish homeland in Palestine where there would be social justice and equality. They referred to each other as the *chaverim* (friends).

A few times a week, Hana would excitedly put on her uniform of blue shorts and white shirt to meet her friends in the local gymnasium for Maccabi Hatzair, an afternoon sports program organized by the youth movement in Prague. Hana formed her closest bonds here. "The mere thought of being with the *chaverim* filled me with bliss, happiness, and joy," she once wrote. Hana's Jewish identity developed within this group. Zionists believed Jews to be a national community, a nation of people with a shared historical language, a territory (ancient Israel), a culture, an ethnicity, and a biological relationship. It wasn't just a religion, and to Hana religion wasn't really a part of it at all. Rather, she daydreamed of being a Jewish pioneer. "Hashomer Hatzair also recruited young people to go to Palestine. This was really influential for me," she told me. "I ate up the Zionism, but I remember my parents were very much against it. They thought it was a lot of propaganda to get European Jews to Palestine. But I loved the camp. I was very idealistic. We made our own mattresses out of straw and slept in a huge tent and had this pioneering mentality. We had one metal dish for every meal. We bathed in the river. There was no running water. We learned Hebrew there."

In September 1938 everything changed for the Czechs and ignoring the threat of Nazism was no longer possible. Hitler wanted Czechoslovakia to cede a German-speaking region called the Sudetenland. He had already annexed Austria and was now threatening a European war if he didn't get what he wanted. So the leaders of Germany, Italy, Great Britain, and France met in Munich and complied with Hitler's demand. They gave away their neighbor in hopes for peace. Czechoslovakia wasn't even invited to attend the negotiations.

A month later the November Pogrom took place in Germany. Dubbed "Kristallnacht"—"The Night of Broken Glass"—it was the first major organized act of violence against the Jewish people during the Holocaust. In just two days, with the encouragement and permission of both the German government and the police force, ordinary citizens smashed and set fire to the German Jewish community. Over 100 synagogues were burned throughout the country, and more than 7,500 stores owned by Jews were destroyed. Books full of Jewish thought—secular and religious, scientific and philosophical—were thrown into piles in town squares and burned, creating a spectacle for bystanders. It was a firsthand education for the children of what would be expected of them in the coming years.

Throughout the winter of 1938–39, the atmosphere in thirteen-year-old Hana's household became tense. Nightly her father turned on the radio, keeping the volume low while listening to the BBC, and nightly Hana would overhear her mother telling him to turn it down so the children wouldn't hear. Dinners were eaten in silence as Emilie and Josef exchanged concerned looks. Both Hana and Petr noticed, but neither understood. Everyone tried to maintain a normal routine, but the atmosphere both inside and outside the home told them that something of great importance was happening.

Six months after the Munich Agreement was signed, the German Army invaded. On March 15, 1939, troops crossed the border in the dead of the night and by morning were marching through Prague in stiff, even rows accompanied by a brass band. My grandmother said the capitulation was unconditional—no blood was shed, no battles were fought. There was no resistance. "It was the beginning of the end."

After the Germans invaded Czechoslovakia, the teachers at Hana's school began to leave. First it was the mathematics professor, then the history professor, then the chemistry teacher—each returned to his or her native country in the middle of the term. "The war came to me when I came to school and it was said that the Jewish students were forbidden," my grandmother told me. "Not 'not permitted,' but *forbidden*. But in the beginning I thought it was fun, almost like a vacation. I helped my mom with the chores. It was like playing hooky." Finally the principal left and the school was pronounced "temporarily closed." Then "temporarily closed" became "permanently closed." Soon after, the Gestapo began using the building as its headquarters.

It wasn't just the closing of the schools that quickly changed everything for Czech Jews—bank accounts were frozen, they were banned from going to the cinema, rations were put on groceries, and professions were restricted, as was owning property. Families were forced to give up their homes, and Hana's father had to give up his store. Many cafés had designated areas where Jews could sit, or displayed signs that declared, No Entry for Jews.

"I remember my parents wanted to immigrate to Uganda," my grandmother reflected. It was one of the countries proposed by the Zionist movement as a possible home for the Jews. "I remember thinking it was the weirdest name. My mother bought herself a knitting machine in order to make a living there. But now, looking back on it, Uganda is a hot country. Why would she want a knitting machine?"

Hana's father dutifully filed and refiled all the necessary paperwork as fast as possible, rushing to get the new forms of identification being issued by the Germans, hoping that his family could get out of Czechoslovakia. When Uganda didn't work out, Josef wrote to distant family members in Cincinnati, pleading for an affidavit so they would have a chance at getting a visa. But by then, walls were being built around borders. In some countries, like Czechoslovakia, the walls kept people in. In other places, like America, the walls were built to keep people out.

My grandmother paused at this point in her story and looked at me with an intensity I hadn't seen when she talked about her childhood. "It's not true, like they say, that Jews marched into concentration camps like sheep to slaughter. People wanted to get out of the country, but nobody, including the Americans, wanted them. You needed exit permits and entrance permits, but nobody wanted the people."

CHAPTER 2

THE START OF AN OBSESSION

It's so important to get away. To gain a different perspective. To see life, as I used to say, through different windows.

—HANA DUBOVÁ, 1985

When I left for Israel at the end of that summer in 2009, my hair was short and blond and my skin was darker than usual. I wore bright-colored shirts and ripped jeans. I always carried a camera. I had absorbed my grand-mother's stories and taken them with me to school in Jerusalem, letting them linger in the back of my mind. I didn't think about them intentionally, nor do I remember processing them on purpose. They were just narratives I layered onto everything I was experiencing.

On one of my first nights at school, I remember sitting on top of a yellow slide in the student village. International students surrounded me. They were from France, Spain, Germany, South Africa, and Canada. They were Christians, Muslims, and Jews. We were all new to the school and had strategically placed ourselves around the communal playground to catch the free Wi-Fi. Smelling the hot air of East Jerusalem, we were full of ego and expectations.

I noticed a guy wearing bright-yellow capris with a matching T-shirt that depicted a cartoon clown vomiting a rainbow. I don't know if he approached me or if I approached him, but we introduced ourselves to each other. I told him that I was "kinda sorta" at school in Philadelphia, but Boston was home. He told me his name was Sergio and that he was studying in London but came from Poznań, a Polish city just a few hours east of Berlin. We began to talk, mostly about music. He promised to make me a playlist in the coming days.

We quickly became each other's first and best friend in Israel. It took me a while to learn the proper spelling of his name, which he taught me was s-e-r-g-i-u-s-z. He told me to stick to calling him Sergio like his other English-speaking friends did, and I told him I would, but that I would still spell it the Polish way. His English was nearly fluent, but his nondescript accent was handicapped by a speech impediment he had picked up when first learning the language. The "th" sound was hard for him as it doesn't exist in Polish, so "three-fourths" came out "fwee-fourfs." He was working on correcting this while perfecting his Hebrew and becoming more fluent in Arabic. He told me that he planned to be a diplomat one day and hoped to work in the Middle East.

I told him that all my grandparents were European also. "My grand-mother, the only one who is still alive, is from Prague," I said. "That's my mom's mom. My mom's dad was from Berlin, but he got out before the war, in 1938. Then my dad's parents were Italian and Danish." Sergiusz told me that he was about as Polish as one could be, but that his last name, Scheller, was German. "My great-grandfather was a Bamber. It was a group of Germans who were invited to settle in the Poznań area back in the 1700s. But they assimilated," he told me. "Borders have changed so much in my part of Europe that it gets confusing sometimes," he said before proudly stating that he had spent the previous summer in the United States working as a waiter in New Jersey. We spent a lot of time talking about our differ-ent countries—past and present. I remember one night, a bit stoned and giggly, we pulled out a map of the world and discussed how wild it was that we were sitting in Asia and that Egypt was a country split across two continents. That was the night that we came up with a grand plan to take a road trip through Jordan. He told me he had been there with his parents and could drive the car and figure out all the logistics.

Sergiusz came from a family of travelers who vacationed in places like Turkey, Tunisia, Egypt, and Italy. That was how he ended up in Israel; he and his parents first visited when he was eighteen and he became fascinated with the country. The more he learned about the region, the more he wanted to understand, and that's what led him to being interested in diplomacy. He tried to explain this to our peers when they asked him why he, a Polish Catholic guy with no Jewish roots, would come to study in Jerusalem. The question became a pressure point for him, and it didn't come just from friends; it came from cab drivers, bartenders, professors. He became resentful about it, especially when he realized that the German students were met with curiosity, while he, a Polish student, was met with suspicion.

We belonged to a multicultural group of students studying in one of the most globally disputed places in the world. Each of us had our own unique reasons for coming to Israel. For Sergiusz it was diplomacy. For me it was photography and escapism. I found myself an internship at a photojournalism agency and spent all my spare time either in the office combing through other people's images or wandering the streets, documenting every unusual and usual sight I saw. I fell in love with the cultural clashes of Jerusalem and the way that history felt personal and present.

That school year, I lived two floors above Sergiusz in the student village. We each lived with a rotating group of roommates and had the type of friendship where we would walk in and out of the other's apartment unannounced. Sometimes Sergiusz and I would get together to watch movies in his bedroom, and sometimes we would snuggle and kiss, but we never talked about it. It was like a secret we were keeping from everyone, including each other. We flirted in other ways too. Sometimes we'd be walking in a crowd of people and by mistake, but not really by mistake, we'd hold each other's hand for several seconds before one of us would pull away. At some point the kissing stopped, except for a drunken night here or there, but our friendship grew.

Together, with our university friends, we watched sunsets from the tops of buildings and sunrises from the tops of mountains. We gathered for Shabbat potluck dinners. We traveled to Jordan and Mitzpe Ramon, to the forests in the north and to the desert in the south, to the Dead Sea, and to the West Bank. We played *futbol* and Frisbee on the grass and on the beach. We went skinny-dipping in the Mediterranean Sea and spent evenings on the roofs of the Old City, overlooking the Western Wall and the Dome of the Rock. We smoked hookah and watched movies dubbed in Hebrew. We showed up at political rallies to expand our minds and laid in the crevices of craters to free them.

We would talk about history and politics and language, trying to outdo each other with memorized facts and lived experiences. Amid this landscape, loaded with thousands of years of conflict and plagued by centuries of war fought in the name of love and belonging, we just were. In our photos, you can't tell that we all spoke different languages, came from different countries, and were raised in different religions. For many of us, our grandparents were once neighbors. What stood between us and them were decades of displacement.

At the end of the school year, I broke down into continuous, heaving sobs the day Sergiusz left Jerusalem to go back to Europe. It was the type of cry that left my face wet and my body exhausted. I longed for him and my life in Israel before it was even gone. He was the first of our group of friends to leave, but soon enough we were all back in our respective countries. I reluctantly returned to Philadelphia so I could graduate from college. It was the summer of 2010. I was twenty-one years old, and the only thing I looked forward to was continuing the storytelling sessions with my grandmother.

We had left off at the point when she had been forced to leave Prague at age fourteen. "My parents gave me two big gifts," she said. "First of all, the gift of life itself; and second, the gift of survival when they sent me away."

Mutti turned eighty-five that July. Her health was failing; we all knew that. Our conversations moved from the balcony to her bed and from a sitting position to a more reclined one. An oil painting of her mother hung above her. I watched the two of them together as I dug my toes into the blanket that covered her frail legs.

The final time my grandmother and I sat together, just the two of us, was on Yom Kippur in 2010. The holiday fell in the middle of September, and I was the family member tasked with driving her to and from the synagogue. She was using a walker now and moved slowly.

I drove us past the mall and toward the house on Ridge Pike in Lafayette

Hill, Pennsylvania, where she had raised her children and where most of my memories as a grandchild lived. We continued straight toward the reform synagogue she attended. I was so used to seeing my grandmother sprightly—in person and in photographs. Despite a lifetime of hiking, swimming, and skiing, her body now required extra time for even the shortest of travels.

The service had already started when we walked into the synagogue. The congregation was full, but we found two seats just near the door. We knew it would be her last time, her final New Year. My grandmother had never been a religious woman, and that was not in spite of or because of the Holocaust. "I think that Judaism is not so much a belief as a tradition I think to do," she said. "I never, ever, was sorry that I am Jewish. Never. Sometimes I was proud of it. But I was never sorry. I was never ashamed of it."

I remember struggling to keep my attention on the group prayer. I wandered outside and sat by a tree with my journal. My grandmother never gave me guilt for taking time for myself. She was fine on her own.

I returned to her in the sanctuary just in time for the Viddui—the prayer of confession. As every year before, the rabbi explained that the prayer is intended to inspire us to understand that all of us bear the burden of our collective sins. Each line, which confesses a wrongdoing, is said in the context of community, not individual action. My grandmother was a woman who loved words deeply, and I imagined her reflecting on the communal aspect of the prayer as she beat her chest like a drum with her fist, as is customary. To my ears, the music made by the shared repentance became a melody of hope, as if saying, "Next year . . . next year we can do better."

On October 8, 2010, Mutti passed away. There were no tubes or sterile walls. There were no doctors dictating visiting hours or nurses checking her vitals. Hana died at home, a place that she had fought, so many times over, to create for herself.

Her body lay peacefully. It was the first time I touched a dead body, but I didn't cry. My memory is in black and white. I remember her skin being cold and soft. I took her hand and kissed it. Surrounding her were her pictures, her writings, and the delicate pages that proved her past. It was everything that I, unknowingly at that time, would come to wrap my world around.

In the years after her death, I uncovered the most beautiful archive of her life. It wasn't a hidden archive or a secret one. It was just what she had left behind. It was everything she had told me, curated and edited. There were preserved albums and hundreds of photographs dating back to the 1920s. There were letters waiting to be translated, journals, diaries, deportation and immigration papers. There were pieces of creative writing from various stages of her life—some marked up with line edits. The archive was seemingly endless. Every time I thought I had found the last box, I discovered another. There were repeated stories—some written at age fourteen, and others at age eighty. There were anecdotes and memories that contradicted each other, bringing the question of memory into all of her stories. There were childhood report cards and souvenirs from her cross-country travels. There were confessions of love, secrets intended to stay private, and flashbacks never intended to be understood.

She had written about being a daughter, a sister, a granddaughter, and a cousin; a friend, a student, and a dedicated member of her youth group. She was a strong-willed teen, a refugee, and an orphan. She was a survivor and a victim, a wanderer and someone who dreamed of home. She was a hopeful immigrant and a forced emigrant. She was an urban dweller and a farmer. She was a pioneer and a storyteller. She was a Czech child, a stateless teen, and an American wife. She was a traveler, an explorer, a teacher, and a student. She spoke six languages. She was a divorcée to one and a reignited flame to another. And for other men, she was the one who got away. She was a bride, a mother, and a grandmother; a young person searching for her future and an elderly person watching her grandchildren search for theirs.

I became obsessed with this material, adopting it as my own and taking it with me when I moved back to Boston after graduating from college. My methods of preserving my grandmother's story would have appalled any professional archivist. These were documents and photographs that should have been handled in a clean environment and stored in boxes that were waterproof and fire-resistant and let in no light. These were delicate, worn pieces of paper, and yet here I was, sitting on my bedroom floor, moving them from one pile to another and storing them in Manila folders with little to no protection.

I digitized and organized it all, plucking it from the past and placing it into my present. I learned my grandmother's handwriting. She used the same shaky cursive to caption her photographs as she did to write letters to friends, while titles were always written in block capitals. I scanned every photograph. I retyped every diary. Every word went from her fingertips to my own.

I paid close attention to the names and places I found in the archive. These details were found on the backs of photographs, on official documents, within the pages of journals, and on stamped letters sent from one country to another. I listed the names chronologically and took note of how she had gotten from one place to another and which train stations she had stopped at. When my grandmother started telling me her story, she said she had felt like she was going on a big adventure. That's what her archive felt like as well.

I began buying books about World War II and the Holocaust. It is the most well-documented genocide from the side of the perpetrators and the victims. I learned the basic facts quickly. World War II began on September 1, 1939 when the Nazis invaded Poland from the west. A few weeks after that, the Soviet Union invaded from the east. The persecution of the Jews started far before that. I taught myself about the roots of anti-Semitism and the rise of the Nazis. It felt like a puzzle. The history books helped me understand my grandmother's story, and my grandmother's story helped me understand the history books.

During these early years of obsession, I shared an apartment in Boston with two friends. I was stringing my rent together by working various jobs—primarily through photography, international travel programs, and teaching. My future felt like it was on the edge of exciting, but not yet burdened. My roommates and I hung white lights around the living room and lit candles while listening to Bob Marley, Kendrick Lamar, and Rudimental. We played games, made friends with each other's friends, and went to concerts. It was that time in life when we were all making bold decisions for ourselves, but not the kind that had to do with kids and marriage. We were all just figuring it out. Barack Obama was president and change was happening. Life was moving and love was flowing.

With each new photograph I scanned or diary entry I transcribed, I became more and more committed to my grandmother's story. It had been almost four years since Hana had died and I'd spent too many years buried in her story to not let it take me somewhere. So I decided I would literally follow in her footprints. I would live in every country she had lived in. I would travel the way she had. I would track down all the characters from her journals, all the names listed in her letters and documents. And most importantly, I would try to find the people who had saved her life. In her diary, my grandmother called the Holocaust an "incomprehensible black page of history." I wanted to know what happens when you turn the page.

Sergiusz and I had kept in touch since our time studying abroad together in Jerusalem, and when I began envisioning a temporary move to Europe to follow my grandmother's story, he was one of the first friends I told. Early in 2014, when I was twenty-five, I let him know I was coming to the Czech Republic with my mom for a family history trip. It would be a "practice run" of sorts before the longer trip I was planning, I explained. He promptly booked a bus ticket to come see me in Prague. It was no big deal, he said. The ride from Warsaw, where he lived, was only twelve hours.

The plan was as such: Sergiusz and I would spend five days together touring Prague, and then my mom would join me in the Czech Republic. He would spend a day with the two of us together and then take the bus back to Poland. Sergiusz gave me that anxious feeling that something good was coming—that type of excitement when your stomach swirls and you can't stop talking. My grandmother had said that traveling and seeing other ways of life would change my life. She said that it would make me stand on my feet and feel more independent. It was her history I was following, but having Sergiusz as a confidant in Europe made it feel like I was embarking on something more.

CHAPTER 3

I BLUSHED IN THE
FACE OF DEATH

He is the only one who is buried in a decent grave.

—HANA DUBOVÁ, 2009

I had already checked into the Airbnb when Sergiusz arrived. It was April 15, 2014. He and I were staying in Žižkov, an eclectic neighborhood in Prague. The last time we had seen one another was two years prior, when we each spent a summer in Israel for work—he at the Polish Embassy in Tel Aviv, and I photographing for a nonprofit. He hugged me tightly and then quickly pulled back.

"I stopped for Kozel," he said. Kozel is a Czech beer that has a funny goat on the label. When I visited Prague the first time, while backpacking in college, it became a favorite of mine. He knew that. "But I put the glass bottles in my backpack, and one broke."

We quickly rescued his laptop from the spill and put the remaining beer in the fridge. Just as we never spoke about our make-out sessions and hand holding in Israel, neither of us acknowledged the months of talking on the phone, the nightly Skype calls, the daily texts, or the recent swapping of *X*s and *O*s that had all led up to this trip. Instead we talked about my upcoming travels. I told him that my mom hadn't been back to Prague since she had visited with my grandmother in 1993. He told me that the country was completely different then, being that it was the year

Czechoslovakia had split into the Czech Republic and Slovakia. I nodded, letting him know I already knew that.

In some ways, Sergiusz knew my history far better than I did, at least from a geopolitical perspective. He loved to talk about it. He was a child born on the cusp of capitalism; he grew up with one foot in the constraints of yesterday and the other in the possibilities of tomorrow. Like Czechoslovakia, Poland gained its independence in 1918 at the end of World War I. And also like Czechoslovakia, it came under communist control after the Second World War and stayed that way until the fall of the Soviet Union in 1989. Although the neighboring countries had similar historical timelines and both had Jewish communities that were nearly eradicated during the Holocaust, Poland, unlike Czechoslovakia, had been heavily bombed by the Nazis. Warsaw especially had been all but razed to the ground.

"*Kawa?*" he asked, holding up a bag of Turkish coffee he had brought with him. The smell reminded us of Israel.

I lay back on the bed—the one that we, just as friends, agreed to share. The walls were a faint yellow, the bedspread was perfectly white, and there were fake flowers in a vase in the corner. Sergiusz set up speakers he had brought with him and put on a playlist he had made, mostly of the songs that we had sent each other in the weeks leading up to this trip.

When the coffee was ready, he brought us each a cup and immediately spilled some on the bedspread.

"*Kurwa!*" he shouted as he ran to get a towel. (Used this way, the Polish *kurwa* is like "fuck" in English.)

"Nervous or something?" I joked.

We cleaned up the spill and drank the rest of the coffee in bed, leaning against each other with a comfortable awkwardness.

"So, you are going to come back this fall?" he asked.

"That's the plan."

"Then you have to come stay with me," he said. "You know, my city, Poznań, is known as 'Berlin's Little Brother' because it survived the war and is close to Germany. It's the best city in our country. I'll be your tour guide."

I leaned further into his body.

He gave my forehead a kiss.

My stomach flipped. Time felt strange—kind of still. The moment felt very cliché, but in a good way. We stared at the wall for a few minutes and let the music play. Disclosure's "Latch" came on. It was the first song he had sent me.

I looked up at him, he looked down at me, and then we kissed. It wasn't heated or passionate. It just was.

He pulled back and stared at me. "Fuck it," he said. "I think I'm in love with you."

I let myself smile. "I think I love you too."

And that was that. We were partners—not boyfriend and girlfriend, but partners.

That first night of our new relationship, we wandered around Prague with three Czech guys (Sergiusz knew one of them) who offered to show us a proper night out. There was homemade *slivovitz* and Czech lager and bars that let us smoke joints inside. We walked through the streets with a massive old-school boom box the guys passed from shoulder to shoulder. As the streets got steeper and my walking became an intoxicated stumble, Sergiusz held my hand. Grand Gothic buildings peered down at me. They made me feel temporary. The great Czech artists and thinkers—Kafka, Mucha, Sudek, Čapek—had all looked up at these buildings. My grandmother had looked up at these buildings. The Nazis, communists, socialists, and democrats had all looked up at these buildings. I felt like I was in another time and place, transported to somewhere between here and there, a moment that knew no decade.

We ended the evening on top of a steep grassy hill. Other groups of people speckled the park. We turned off the boom box. The conversations around me were all in a language I didn't understand. In the distance, we could see church spires, the Old Town Square, and the Vltava River. I leaned close to Sergiusz and whispered in his ear, "Isn't it wild that this is where my grandmother comes from?"

Five days later, Sergiusz went back home to Poland, and my mom and I stepped into the landmarks of her mother's past. We went to museums and synagogues. We sat in cafés and admired classic Czech art. We met distant family members and even spent Shabbat with a few of them. Some had only recently learned that they were Jewish. We seemingly knew more about their family history than they did.

We also visited Kolín, the small Bohemian town where my grandmother was born. We were treated like esteemed guests there. The mayor publicly acknowledged our visit; a photographer followed us around and journalists repeatedly asked us about how it felt to be back in the place where our family had once lived. My mom and I had completely different answers. I felt fascination. She felt loss. "Like a phoenix rising from the ashes," she told one reporter. "It's so cool to be here," I told another one. We were the proof that Jews did in fact once have a home here. We were living, breathing memorials. For my mom it was tragic, and for me it was redemptive. It's amazing how much difference one generation makes.

I took my own photos as well, documenting my mom being documented. I took a series of pictures as she cleaned pollen off an old headstone that belonged to my great-great-grandfather. He was the only one of Hana's grandparents to have been given a dignified death. She once wrote, "My grandfather died at the age of sixty-five. He was laid out on his bed, and we children were asked to kiss him goodbye, he still had jet-black hair, which I always thought was from the coal. He is the only one of the entire family who had a funeral and a grave. We planted a blue spruce at his grave site. The rest of the family was eventually murdered in concentration camps."

During this visit, we were invited to stay in an old school that used to belong to the Jewish community and was just a stone's throw away from the synagogue. We were told that neither building was used very often. It was as if they had been dusted off just for us.

After Kolín, we went to Theresienstadt, a concentration camp not far from Prague where over 30,000 Jews died and another 140,000 were imprisoned before being sent "further east," a euphemism for death camps such as Auschwitz-Birkenau, Treblinka, Majdanek, and Sobibor. It was the first of such places Hana's family was sent upon deportation. A local journalist set us up with a guide who showed us which building my family had been kept in and walked us through the crematorium, the mass graves, and the cemetery. He took us into the barracks and stayed close by as we stood in the large, cold rooms where prisoners had slept on bare planks of wood. The guide explained that many people would sleep in the same bunk. In the ghetto's museum, a welcome center of sorts, my mom and I found the name of my grandmother's brother painted on a wall that listed the children who were victims—Petr Dub, 1929–1942.

Sergiusz texted me love notes when I was in each of these places. I blushed in the face of death because I felt loved.

―――――――――

I officially relocated to Europe in the fall of 2014—September 29 to be exact. That night, I boarded a plane in Boston, carrying a backpack of belongings and a suitcase of camera gear, to go in pursuit of my grandmother's memory.

I would first stay in Poland with Sergiusz for a month. In anticipation of my arrival, Sergiusz got himself a studio apartment in a neighborhood called Kabaty. It was right on the edge of the city—the last stop on the subway line, which made it easy for me as I never had to worry about where to get off. We nested our one-room abode, making it our own. He immediately integrated me into his world by introducing me to his friends and fulfilling his promise to take me to his parents' home in Poznań.

While I was there, he helped me file the paperwork that would allow for me to stay in Europe for the year. I had tried to get a visa for my professional work, but there was no box to check for "aspiring journalist taking deep dive into family history." So instead, Sergiusz's family, who I hadn't even met yet, vouched for me financially. And at the appropriate government offices, Sergiusz and I expressed our plans to marry in the near future. It was because of him that I could follow Hana's story.

I felt guilty letting him help me. I felt guilty having the relationship we did. My grandmother had been alone, so I felt like I, too, had to be alone. It didn't feel right that Sergiusz was giving me a home base. He was someone to come back to, someone to support me, and someone to miss.

I pushed these thoughts aside, knowing well enough that my feelings of guilt were stupid.

Regardless of these feelings, our relationship was really solid right away. We had almost five years of friendship behind us before we started dating and quickly found a rhythm as a couple. It was just as easy when I moved in with him as when we had a long-distance relationship. He supported my comings and goings and even helped me with logistics. We shared the same interests, we liked the same books, and we socialized the same way. I've always been someone who has loved being alone, but I loved being with him more.

That's not to say we always agreed. Our first fight happened the morning we went to Auschwitz. It was mid-October, just around our six-month anniversary. Sergiusz had visited the notorious Nazi concentration and death camp many times before, but for me it was like a rite of passage. If I was going to tell a story about the Holocaust, I had to visit Auschwitz, especially if I was in Poland.

Our visit didn't begin well. Sergiusz hadn't confirmed our hostel reservation in Kraków, so at the last minute, we had to find a place to sleep that we could afford. The next morning, the day we were going to Auschwitz, his alarm didn't go off, so we started the day rushing. I was cranky without coffee and found myself in a deep pit of despair and anger for relying on another person. I lectured myself about needing to do things on my own. I was battling my relationship with independence and self-sufficiency now that I was in a serious partnership. It was a personal demon I hadn't needed to confront when we were still long-distance. When she was sixty, my grandmother once wrote in her journal, "At home I'm often alone . . . I don't have to be alone, but there is always an overture, an effort on my side." I thought about those words like heeding a warning: Don't be scared of the effort. You don't need to be alone.

On the streets of Kraków, I was unable to compose myself. Sergiusz and I made a scene full of tears and frustrated shouting. I felt like a horrible person. We were going to a factory of mass murder, a place where children were ripped from their mothers' arms, where hair was shaved off, where gold teeth were stolen, where youth didn't exist no matter the age, where

Jews were forced to assist in the murder of their fellow Jews, where neighbors had to kill neighbors, where a piece of moldy bread was the difference between life and death, where the entire moral code was dark, repugnant, and unfathomable. In Auschwitz-Birkenau, more than 1.1 million Jews, seventy thousand Poles, twenty-five thousand Romani and some fifteen thousand prisoners of war from the Soviet Union and other countries were murdered. And yet, we were fighting because we had overslept.

We boarded a local bus from Kraków to Oświęcim, the small town where the Nazis had built Auschwitz in 1940. We squeezed in the back corner, where I could lay my head against the window and watch the forests that lined the highway. Most of the other passengers, some of whom had to stand in the aisle, appeared to be locals. I assumed the ones with cameras were also tourists. The radio played pop music. We passed by an H&M, a McDonald's, and a Biedronka, the largest supermarket chain in Poland.

The bus ride calmed me and Sergiusz, and our fight resolved itself as quickly as it had begun. We whispered that we weren't really mad at each other. "I've never had someone to be that emotional with," I told him. "It felt kind of healthy."

"I trust you so much," he replied.

I put my earphones in. Sergiusz sat quietly next to me, his hand on my upper thigh. On occasion, I would move my head to his shoulder. I loved him so much it scared me. I drifted between my own world and wondering what identity meant for those raised in the shadow of Auschwitz's infamy.

We neared our stop about an hour into the ride. I removed my earphones to hear Ricky Martin's "Livin' La Vida Loca" playing on the radio. I gave Sergiusz a look. He understood it right away. *What the fuck?* his face told me. *Really? "Livin' La Vida Loca" as we arrive at Auschwitz?* We got off on the side of the highway with a couple of other passengers and walked toward the entrance of the camp. The closer we got, the more people we saw. There were hundreds of tourists speaking different languages. History brought diversity to Poland—at least to this place.

In the camp's museum, we peered into the protective glass cases that displayed prisoners' suitcases, shoes, and family pictures. We stared at the combs and hairbrushes, the pocket watches and wedding rings, the menorahs, candlesticks, and pages of the prayer book. I was taken aback by Sergiusz's seriousness. I wondered if he felt the catastrophic core of this place—the lingering ghosts of the hunted—more than I did.

The process of selection and murder was well thought out here. In fact, everything the Nazis did was intentional and organized. Men and boys were separated from the women and girls. Some were chosen to work; others were chosen to die. The ones chosen for death were sent to Birkenau, the second camp, about three kilometers away. They were ordered to undress so they could be disinfected. Then they were locked in a chamber and suffocated by gas. Their bodies were incinerated in the crematorium. Their bones were pulverized. Their ashes were scattered. This happened over and over again, every single day. I read the captions and plaques that accompanied the artifacts with the same stoicism I had when reading the history books that prepared me for my visit.

On the bus between Auschwitz and Birkenau, we observed a group of high school students from Spain munching on bags of chips and tossing ham and cheese sandwiches to each other. They chatted happily. Sergiusz sat next to me, somber, as he did his best to ignore their behavior.

We walked along the worn train tracks in Birkenau, passing the freight cars used for deportations. The sky was perfectly blue, and the day was warm for October. My family wasn't deported here, as far as I knew. But it didn't matter. It didn't change their fate. Sergiusz stayed close to me as I set up my tripod and filmed the trees. Their roots grew strong in spite of the death that fed the soil. I stared at them, thinking that my own roots were not so different.

We didn't talk. Sergiusz wouldn't hold my hand, nor I his. He only whispered to me, "These people, their grandchildren—they could have been my neighbors."

Back in Kraków that night, Sergiusz and I went to a restaurant called Klezmer-Hois in the former Jewish district, which was experiencing a kind of renaissance. We listened to live klezmer music and ordered "Sabbath Soup," schnitzel with beets and red cabbage, and "Purim Chicken." We began the meal with vodka shots.

When Sergiusz got up to use the bathroom, I looked at the art on the walls. It depicted religious men from the shtetl with their big beards and Torah studies—a part of Jewish life that had become folkloric to me. I felt like they were both critiquing me and watching over me with care. I stared into their painted eyes and felt them stare back. The music kept playing. For the first time that day, I felt that those who were dead were once alive.

CHAPTER 4

DON'T FORGET WHERE
YOU COME FROM

When I was young and my father spoke about World War I, I thought it was ancient history even though it ended only seven years before I was born. Whatever preceded 1925 didn't concern me.

—HANA'S DIARY, 1990

In 1998, while giving a recorded testimony about the Holocaust, my grandmother was asked if there were any decisions she made in her life that could be traced back to her wartime experiences. She quickly responded, "I don't know about decisions, but I know that I am extremely independent. I made my own decisions. I take my own consequences. When my grandchildren say this isn't fair, life isn't fair, I say, 'Nobody told you life is fair. Life is not fair. But you have to deal with it.'"

It was by virtue of being in the Zionist youth movement that Hana was able to get out of Nazi-occupied Czechoslovakia. She told me it was like receiving a winning lottery ticket. She was accepted into a program called Hakshara—meaning preparation—for Jewish teens who wished to go to Palestine. "That is, if the British would allow it," she pointed out. The British had taken control of Palestine during the First World War after seizing it from the Ottoman Empire and were permitting Jewish immigration, but in limited numbers. The first and most urgent step was for the chosen *chaverim* to get out of Czechoslovakia and, in Hana's case, go to Denmark.

The Danish government collaborated with the Zionist movement and an organization called the Women's International League for Peace and Freedom to coordinate the arrival of the Jewish teens, all of whom were between the ages of fourteen and sixteen. The plan was that each teen would be given a six-month contract with a Danish foster family who lived in the countryside. In exchange for work, they would receive room and board. "The idea was, 'Let's get these kids out of Czechoslovakia and to Palestine,'" my grandmother explained to me. "'Let us come to Denmark to learn Hakshara—to learn agriculture—and then go on to Palestine from there.'"

Hana's mother took her to a doctor to get the necessary shots and helped her pack. Her father filed every necessary form and listed everything he would give her when she would leave. He promised the Nazis to relinquish the dowry and inheritance Hana was entitled to and stood with her to obtain an exit permit that would be stamped in her new passport issued by the German Reich. Hana's brother, Petr (often called Peta), was too young to be eligible for the program, so he would stay in Prague.

"The war will be over soon," her parents repeated over and over before letting go of Hana on the train station platform. "Be a good girl. Don't forget where you come from." They kissed her cheeks repeatedly, adjusting her coat and tightening her scarf, making sure she had all of her belongings. It was October 1939, just a month after the war had officially begun.

I imagine her departure like a scene from a black-and-white silent film of loved ones desperately waving to each other as the train pulls away. Hana waves from the window, her head peeking out as her mother wipes her eyes with a handkerchief. Her father has one hand on his wife's waist and the other on his son's shoulder as his daughter disappears into history. Grief fills the station like a thick fog.

I imagine all of the parents on the platform exchanging glances, seeking approval from each other. They need to know that they're doing the right thing by saying goodbye. They need to believe it's safer to send their children into the unknown than to have them stay home.

———————

I followed Hana out of Prague. After a month in Poland with Sergiusz, I took the same bus ride to the Czech Republic as he had taken half a year before. I checked into a hostel early in the morning and stayed for a couple days before boarding a train at Prague's main railway station. I traveled through the Czech countryside and into Germany. I was going to do it exactly as my grandmother had done—swiftly and with few belongings—guided by the words found in her archive. I would switch trains in Berlin and head to Warnemünde, a coastal town in Germany, like she did.

> *I'm writing in the train, from the train station in Berlin . . . The transfer went quite well except the heavy backpack . . . We went from one train terminal to another by subway. They even have double-decker buses here.*
>
> —OCTOBER 11, 1939

Then I would cross the Baltic Sea by boat, like she did.

> *I'm almost at my destination. The boat ride was very nice. We examined the entire ship, even the engine room.*
>
> —OCTOBER 12, 1939

And then take a train from the coast of Denmark to Copenhagen, like she did. No one checked my passport or asked me where I was going.

> *Today I want to write a detailed letter . . . When we arrived in Warnemünde, some of us had to get totally undressed at customs and some only had their luggage examined. We were not allowed to open our backpacks until upon arrival in Warnemünde. I was among those whose luggage was examined. I didn't have to get undressed. Our escort took us to Warnemünde, and then we were alone on the ship.*
>
> —OCTOBER 13, 1939

I also had a piece of writing Hana wrote in 2004 about fleeing Czechoslovakia. She wrote it when she took a class called "Memories and Memoirs." She called the piece "Stepping Stones in My Life":

Getting off at the Main Station [in Copenhagen], the first sign which caught my eyes was "TELEFON & TELEGRAF."

Hurrah. Hurrah.

This foreign language cannot be so different from my own.

I find solace and comfort in uttering aloud these two words. They sound so familiar, although I am aware that I am not at home here.

The train ride was suspenseful, strenuous, and mainly very scary and, oh, so sad.

It was only yesterday I boarded a train in a familiar train station, from where we so often traveled to my grandparents to celebrate holidays and other occasions. It was only a one-hour train ride.

But this time I sat alone on the train for hours, crossing different countries. Papers being examined by passport control's sourly officials, giving me dirty looks, stamped and handed back to me with a sneer.

How much anxiety, energy, and wait was spent in obtaining this document, which does not even have my proper nationality or my name. My father and I stood 48 hours in front of the Gestapo Headquarters in a miles-long line to obtain an exit permit for me, stamped in the issued passport. And then we found out that it is a German passport marked "Protektorat Böhmen und Mähren" (Protectorate of Bohemia and Moravia) as we already were under Nazi occupation and had lost our independence. My name was not HANA but SARA, as all the Jewish females were renamed Sara, and the Jewish males Israel. The passport cover and all the following pages had a huge red *J* across them, indicating *Jude* (Jew).

Every time the train stopped for this or that control, I trembled handling my passport. Am I going to reach my goal? Am I going to be arrested? Am I going to be sent back home?

Changing trains in Berlin, there was a physical examination of my private parts, in case I was hiding jewelry or precious stones, which they confiscated long ago.

Back, back home. In a way I wished I could see my parents and my brother once more. It was only yesterday that we all stood on the platform of Wilson Station. We were all trying bravely to keep a stiff upper lip. Embracing, kissing, hugging, embracing, kissing again and again. Last minute advice, "Be a good girl," "Know where you come from."

Goodbye, goodbye, goodbye.

The war will be over soon, and you'll come home.

I was 14 years old.

I found out the Danish language has absolutely no similarity to Czech.

But I was safe and saved.

There is a friend from Prague that Hana doesn't mention in this particular story, but he became a leading character when she retold it to me. His name was Dáša (pronounced "DAH-sha"), and she was smitten with him. Their families were friends, and sometimes Dáša and his father would come to Hana's house to play Ping-Pong in the evenings. Both teens were involved in the Zionist youth movement, and when they went to summer camp in Bezpráví in the summer of 1939, Dáša flirted with Hana by doing things like smearing shoe polish on her face while she was sleeping. They had their first kiss on her fourteenth birthday. The story goes that Hana dropped her fork under the table, and when she went down to get it, Dáša met her underneath and kissed her. "I was madly in love with him," she told me.

By the time Hana and Dáša learned they would be leaving Czechoslovakia for Denmark, they were already something of a couple. "I really wanted to be near him in Denmark," Hana said. "So I switched. I switched with another girl so I could be with him. But I was punished for that because we were way away from the other children. The other children were placed in farms where they could meet each other."

From Copenhagen, Hana and Dáša traveled north together to a town called Gørløse while many of the other *chaverim* went to a city in the south called Næstved. When they got off the train, they were met by a local priest and teacher. The priest was tall and wore a robe with a lace collar and a stovepipe hat. Mr. Larson, the teacher, was shorter and spoke German. He told them that Dáša was assigned to live with his family; they would all go to his house for a dinner of raisin soup and liver sausages, and the family with whom Hana would be living would join them there.

Hana wrote home a few days later, on October 15:

My dear ones,

As I wrote you in my last letter, I'm with Dáša in the same village. But I'm outside of the village, and Dáša lives in the school. It's really wonderful here, and I have it better than I ever could have imagined or wished for. I have my own room. The only thing that is missing is a wardrobe, but behind a curtain I have some hooks and a washbasin and two shelves for my underwear. I get woken up at 7:30, get up at 7:45, and at 8:00 I'm dressed and ready for breakfast. I eat bread and drink coffee. At 9:00 workers come in from the fields and they get a breakfast of butter, lard, marmalade, salami, and bread, and the table is set with coffee cake. By the way, dear Mami [Hana's mother], I gave them the coffee cake you baked for them, and they thank you very much, but as you see, it wasn't necessary. There is also ham with mustard, cheese, white bread, dark bread, and French bread. We can help ourselves to as much as we desire. There is also milk, tea, and heavy cream. After breakfast I wash and dry the dishes, then it's time to prepare the midday meal. I clean my room, sweep and dust the living and dining rooms, and wash the floors with a rag on a stick. After the meal, I put the one-year-old to bed. I was wrong when I wrote that they have a 20-year-old here. It is the farm worker who is that old. The children's ages are as follows: Jan, 8½ years old; Hans, 7 years old; sister, 6 years old; and one-year-old Paul. Then I take the midday meal to the workers in the fields. Then I wash out my clothing, as neither the suitcase nor the trunk have arrived yet. Dáša then comes and teaches me to ride the bicycle, or I go to the village (Gørløse). At 6:00 I return and prepare supper, which is similar to breakfast. After supper the men play cards and Mrs. Greve [the farmer's wife] and I put little Paul to bed, and then the other children go to sleep. It's now 7:30 p.m. Then Mrs. Greve starts on her mending, and I read. Between 8:00 and 9:00 p.m. I heat up some water and go to my room where I was myself by candlelight, which is almost gone as I got a little candle stub, but they have promised me a kerosene lantern. I read some more in my bed. I say my prayers, praying especially for you all, and go to sleep. I sleep till 7:30 a.m. and start all over again.

What do you conclude about my days? You can reach only one conclusion, and that is that I have it too good, as if I were at home. Please write a lot and in detail. You know I'm interested in everything that's going on at home.

Peta: Did you start school? How do you like it? Who is your teacher? I must end as there is no more room on this paper which was given to me.

Your devoted daughter,
Hana

Her parents wrote a letter dated the following day, October 16, 1939:

Write all the details. Tell us how you like it there and what kind of people they are. What kind of work do you do, and is it a large farm where you are? Are you all alone . . . or with someone else? What kind of village is it, small or big? We are curious about everything, but mainly how you like it and if the people are nice to you. We all miss you . . . Saturday Babicka [grandmother] Dubová arrived . . . Now she'll stay here with us. Today Jirka Grimm [Hana's peer] went for his exit permit, so hopefully

the second group [of chaverim] will depart soon. Eva Levy [another peer]
left with her family for Palestine . . . I am asking you to write neater, as
we are going to save all your letters.

Hana's new home had no running water and no electricity. Every day,
she pumped water from the well in the courtyard to bring into the house
and heat on the stove. Twice a day, she prepared oatmeal covered with
cream and sugar for the family. In the evening, a brick would be put in
the stove, then removed and wrapped with newspaper to be taken to bed
as a source of warmth in her unheated room. The breath she released as
she slept became sheets of ice on her blanket. She wore wooden shoes akin
to Dutch clogs given to her by the farmer which she stuffed with straw
and newspaper in the winter. She was also given a pair of rubber boots to
be worn in the barn. "The farmer expected me to know something, but I
didn't even know that milk came from cows," she told me. "I thought it
came from the milkman—that's how we always got it in Prague: delivered
to the door in a glass jar. But you learn."

Hana learned how to milk the cows and take care of the chickens and
the hen house. She told me it was complete immersion. She helped with
the pig slaughter and learned how to make sausages and Danish blood
pudding, called *blodpølse*. She washed the family's clothes in a manual
washing machine and, with each turn of the handle, taught herself a new
Danish word or some Hebrew vocabulary. And when she folded the sheets,
the tablecloths, and the pillow cases, she sang herself Danish songs.

Every couple of weeks, she would bike to meet Dáša in the woods. His
name is all over the pages of her diary during this time. Her feelings for him
waver. Her need for him wavers. On some pages, she reflects about being
independent, and on others, she declares her love for him. One particular entry I love is from the spring of 1940: "One day we were lying next
to each other in some small woods, and I am convinced that he, too, was
very happy. He was telling me that he liked me very much and that I am
pretty and have smooth cheeks and all the things that a person in love can
say. I was saying nothing, just listening."

In another entry she writes:

On January 3, under the Christmas tree in the gymnasium, Dáša was sitting next to me . . . He kept looking up at the gallery where his farmer's daughter was sitting and whom he was crazy about. He kept saying: "Look, Hanka, how Karen keeps winking at me." I thought it was a joke. I even followed him up to the gallery, where he went to see Karen, and pretended I was looking for a handkerchief in my coat. Then he took a cigarette he was offered and struck a match to light it. And I could no longer take it: "Stop it, Dáša!" He spat at me in response in front of all the people!? Still, I wasn't upset at him. I still liked him, but this really offended me. He then saw me home in a snowstorm and in the dark. I walked arm in arm with him and was content. Everything was okay again.

Regardless of their on-and-off-again relationship, Hana and Dáša shared postage and sent letters home together, all of which were censored by the Germans. Words were blacked out, and each envelope was stamped with a swastika, the Nazi seal of approval, but at least both the children and the parents knew their loved ones were alive and seemingly well. Dáša once wrote,

Dearest Parents,

I hope that the Dubs will be so kind as to give you this letter. As Hanka wrote, we have it very good here, so do not worry about us. In communicating I am much better than Hana, as the teacher speaks some German . . .

Your loving son, Dáša

Hana and Dáša would meet with the other *chaverim* as often as possible, often gathering at a small house in the forest near Næstved. Here they could gossip in their native language, flirt with each other, compare their progress with learning Danish and Hebrew, and exchange news from back home. They celebrated major Jewish holidays together and daydreamed about traveling on to Palestine.

On April 9, 1940, Denmark was forced to join the war. German soldiers occupied their northern neighbor under the pretext of safeguarding them from a British invasion. Hana, Dáša, and the other Czech teens found themselves under Nazi control yet again. The soldiers trod lightly on the Copenhagen cobblestones and across the flat farmland, administering a relatively mild occupation. Hitler believed Denmark, with its Germanic roots, to be a natural ally and an example of how life could look under Nazi world order. So the Germans allowed the Danish government to remain in power, and civil institutions were left intact, including the constitution.

The Danish king, Christian X, maintained rule and often rode his horse around Copenhagen to demonstrate resistance against the Nazi occupation. Throngs of cyclists and pedestrians would follow him in a parade of Danish solidarity. The king publicly stated that all those living in the country—Danes and immigrants alike—would be protected, and when the German government demanded that all Jews be registered, the request was denied under the pretext that the Danish constitution forbade discrimination on the basis of religion. No group of people was to be subjected to unusual treatment. The Danish government could have chosen to protect solely Danish Jews. They had no legal responsibility to protect the refugees, but no distinction was made. Germany's discriminatory policies had the unintended effect of unifying the Danes against them.

Back in Prague, Hana's father, Josef, was still fighting to immigrate to America. Worried that he, Emilie, and Petr wouldn't be able to leave Europe, he wrote to Hana, pleading with her to go to the American embassy in Copenhagen to see if the affidavit he requested from the distant family in America had come through. He also wrote to the American consulate asking them to send his daughter a visa application.

Hana refused, declaring to herself that she would never leave her friends. On August 6, 1940, she wrote in her diary,

I sent both letters back and also a letter saying that I didn't give a damn about the affidavit and that I had to go to Eretz [the land of Israel]—that's what I sent to the American consulate in Copenhagen. Then they left me alone, except for one phone call . . . Still, Daddy kept bombarding me with letters . . . Then Daddy hit the roof, reproaching me for not loving my own parents, leaving them high and dry, and [mentioning] how much they had sacrificed for me, and me nothing for them, and that I was an ungrateful daughter and how they should disown me. From their point of view, they are completely right. But I am young and want to create something, want to face life for what it is, to build and help even with hard work. I don't want to go to Cincinnati to stay with my rich great-great-aunt to study and live a cushy life. No, that's not my ideal.

In the six months after Denmark was occupied, the deportations to Auschwitz began. Germany invaded Belgium and the Netherlands and occupied Paris. The Lodz Ghetto in Poland was sealed, imprisoning 164,000 Jews in a four-square-kilometer space. Communication between neighbors, friends, and family went from being censored to being dangerous. And the Blitz on England began with Germany attacking London for fifty-seven days straight. In the first day alone, over three hundred tons of bombs hit the city.

Hana didn't know any of this. It was quiet in the countryside, with no more than a rare radio broadcast to tell the news. As far as she knew, Palestine was still possible, as was returning to Prague. On November 19, 1940, she wrote a piece in her diary titled "My World." It is a moment of war seen through the eyes of a hopeful teen:

Sometimes it feels so cold and uninviting and damp, when the rain soaks through the walls all the way to my bed. But on Saturday, when I wash the doorstep, mop the floor, and tidy everything up, I think that even a king has not such a beautiful bedroom . . . The table has one compartment with books I am reading, newspapers, [my] journal, and a comb . . . Next to it, my satchel. Then a suitcase covered with an old blanket on which I sit no matter what I am doing. Next to the trunk is a little table with a framed family photograph and a chair, then a cupboard on which there is a sewing kit, ointments, a flashlight, and various knickknacks. Next to it, pegs with work clothes and all that I wear. On the walls hang my Magen David—the Star of David—and a framed picture of Bezpráví. I am going to add pictures of my parents and Peta . . . This is my room. My world where I rule. The world which I trust and confide in. These walls have seen so much—so much sorrow, so much joy. And the window? That's the most beautiful part. Leaning out of it or sitting on the floor . . . looking out at night. Watching the stars. I cannot see the moon. It is true that not a single sunny ray ever wanders in here, nor the moonlight at night, but the stars, those I like best of all planets; those I can see. I can see them and hear a song buzzing in my mind: ". . . Where are you, my star?" Is it true that people's destinies are written in the stars? What do they say about me? I don't know. But I am not afraid! Even if it is no good, I have to face it. Sometimes I don't think this way, and there are no stars outside. It is dark outside and in my window too. Then I turn back to the light of my room. My cozy room that contains me, comforts and soothes me. I know that you won't disclose anything about me, my dear world. My impossible desires, my hot tears, my strange thoughts, my writing and letters torn into pieces. I know I can trust you. I can be safe with you, in you. This is why I sometimes all too happily put myself in bed and know that you won't allow anything bad to happen to me.

CHAPTER 5

THE PEOPLE WERE KIND

All those things one once had and took for granted become so precious when we lose them, and then we are sorry for not acknowledging them and not making the most of them. The same goes for me. Only now that I am abroad, I can see what motherly love meant to me. Not that I wouldn't be independent or miss her helpful hands at work; no, there is something else that's lacking, and that's a mother herself. I think that especially at my age, when I am growing up, I need a mother the most.

—HANA'S DIARY, 1940

In 2012 a man named Knud-Arne Nygaard was reading his local paper in Næstved, Denmark, when he came across an article about young Czech refugees during World War II. He didn't think much about it until a few days later when he was visiting his mother, who was in her nineties. Sitting in her home, it dawned on him that maybe these children were part of a story she had told many times—the story about a Jewish girl named Hana.

Knud-Arne wrote to the journalist right away, a local reporter named Jan Jensen. Jan put Knud-Arne in touch with a Czech journalist named Judita Matyášová who had done the research Jan's article was based on. For many years Judita had been working on a documentary project that explored the fate of the group of teens my grandmother fled Czechoslova-kia with in 1939. Knud-Arne asked Judita if there happened to be a girl in the group named Hana Dubová. She responded quickly that yes, there was a girl by that name, but she had passed away. "However," she said to him, "there is family of hers in Boston."

Knud-Arne's mother, Jensine, was not much older than Hana when the war began. She married her husband, Arne, in April 1940, the same month Germany had occupied Denmark. Her mother-in-law, Karen Nygaard, was an active member of the Women's International League for Peace and Free-dom, the organization that helped Hana and the other *chaverim* get out of Czechoslovakia. Karen and her husband had fourteen children themselves and had begun taking in refugee children from the start of the war, first from Finland and then from Czechoslovakia. Their attitude was, "There is always room for one more." So when Jensine and Arne moved to their own farm as newlyweds, they too took in young refugees. It was a big part of their family story, and Jensine talked about it whenever the war was brought up; Knud-Arne had heard about it his entire life.

Judita gave Knud-Arne my mom's email address, and he immediately wrote to introduce himself. "My mother never knew what had happened to Hana after the war," he told her. "But they corresponded a couple times. My mother saved her letters and talked about Hana quite often. This story has always been with me. As a kid, when you hear that kind of story several times, it grows in you and becomes an important part of who you are."

My mother's adrenaline soared with this news. She didn't need as much sleep as she was used to and woke up excited to exchange emails with Knud-Arne, hoping that every new detail about his mother's life would bring her closer to her own history. Soon after making the connection, my mom, accompanied by my father, traveled to Denmark to meet Jensine. She wanted to thank her for being one of the reasons our family was alive. The two met for the first time in the fall of 2012. My mom said that meeting Jensine and her family was like "walking through a threshold of incredible love and gratitude." They embraced each other for a long time, holding each other and kissing one another's cheeks. Knud-Arne, who translated during the visit, said, "To put names and faces behind all that I had heard about for sixty years—that was amazing. For my mother, meeting Janet was as if seeing Hana herself, like meeting an old acquaintance from her youth."

I went to meet Jensine a year later. She was ninety-three years old and frail yet sturdy, as I imagined an elderly farmer would be. I wish I could say that I found Jensine's family myself, but it was Knud-Arne's curiosity that brought them to me. I remember walking into his home and seeing old family photos framed on his wall. There was a portrait of his parents on their wedding day. It had the same sepia tone as so many in Hana's archive. His dining room table was set with a traditional Danish lunch spread— smoked herring, salmon, rye bread, hard-boiled eggs, Danish meatballs called *frikadeller*, Carlsberg beer, and schnapps for a toast. I was with my mom, my dad, Judita, and her film crew. Cameras and microphones captured our words and expressions as our two families swapped stories.

"Always, since I was a kid, I have been very interested in this story," Knud-Arne said. "It's a fantastic story. It has drama and everything in that story. And this meant a lot to my mother—we wanted her to tell the story, and the grandchildren wanted to hear about it. Everybody heard about the Holocaust and what happened to the Jews. It was a good story that in our family there was a Jew living and escaping afterwards."

In the months before Hana moved in with Jensine, she was living with a woman she regularly referred to as the "Old Witch." She wrote diary entries like, "the Old Witch doesn't like it when I speak without being asked," and, "the Old Witch didn't let me do anything useful—nothing I could learn, only the dirty work." It had been over a year since Hana had moved away from Dáša in Gørløse and closer to the other *chaverim* in Næstved, and in that time, small groups of the Czech teens were being sent to Palestine. I am not certain whether their journeys were legal, as the British, who controlled Palestine, had severely limited Jewish immigration when they issued the White Paper of 1939. My grandmother told me her luggage was sent with a group, but that she was not. "Why don't they send us in one group, as we would like, as they promised? Why are they sending us to Eretz so broken up?" she wrote in her diary in February 1941. "What else could save me but aliyah [moving to Palestine]? And how will that turn out? In what order are we going to go? How are we going to travel? We don't know. We are helpless, and we have to do what we are told. Ordered around, commanded. With much patience we have to bear all the insults, scolding, and mistreatment. With a bitter smile on our lips, we listen to ourselves being bad-mouthed," she wrote in April.

Knowing that some of her peers had moved from their farms and left for Palestine, Hana wrote to the women's organization that coordinated her homestay and asked if she could live with a different family. Getting her wish, Hana moved to Jensine's home in the summer of 1941, just a few days after she turned sixteen. "My parents were contacted saying that there was a girl who wasn't satisfied with her host family and asked if she could come live with them; they said okay, and that girl was Hana," Knud-Arne recounted. "Hana was a big help for my mother. It was a good situation for everyone."

Jensine was twenty-one years old when Hana moved in. She and Arne lived in Holme-Olstrup, a small village about ten kilometers from Næstved, with their baby boy, named Mogens. Hana's work routine at the new farm was simple. She woke up at 5:30 to make the coffee and prepare slices of bread with butter and honey. After she had breakfast with Jensine and Arne, she cleaned the house, took care of Mogens, and tended to chores on the farm. She was always invited to join the family for holidays, meals, and celebratory gatherings. "Even though I might have been in the pigsty ten minutes before washing my hands, I was considered part of the family," my grandmother once said. She had been in Denmark for almost two years, but for the first time, she felt like she belonged.

Hana continued to exchange letters with her parents throughout the summer of 1941, but then, according to her archive, the letters stopped. In one of her final letters home, she wrote,

Dearest Parents,

    Our little boy is Mogens. He is three months old. I feed him, I cook for him, sometimes I dress him. I can do it almost like a real mother. Please don't laugh at me for saying this. But really, I can imagine that one day I will have someone like him . . . Yesterday I worked in the field. I was there alone, and I was thinking, "What a

big land!" I hear machines working not far from me in another field.
I hear the train behind the highway. I see seagulls flying above me. I
see thousands of raspberries. I know I have to work, but sometimes I
just lie down for a few minutes and enjoy all around, observing all
around. Oh, God, how beautiful it is. Always the same, but different.
It goes so quietly, like yesterday, like a week before, a month before,
years before. Nothing is changing here, but not far from here is blood,
and thousands of "heroes" are dying. "Heroes"? They are victims of
war, corpses of nations. And at home? Oh, my God. But now I wake
up and sing. I have to be at home in time, at five o'clock. I just turned
my head and see what I did in the field. All this is my work; I am so
proud of it. I am sixteen, and I can do so many things.

I miss you all,
Hana

When I decided to follow my grandmother's story, I reached out to
Knud-Arne to ask if any of his family members would host me. I told him
that I wanted to work on a Danish farm like my grandmother had done.
He said I wouldn't find a farm like they had in the 1940s, but that his niece,
Sine, would have the closest thing to it. So I wrote to Sine and introduced
myself as Hana's granddaughter. I explained that I was a photographer from
Boston following Hana's story and that I wanted to live with her and work
on her farm, like my grandmother did for Jensine. In exchange, I wanted
to photograph my time. Without any questions, Sine agreed.

I flew to Denmark in February 2015. Sergiusz and I officially became
engaged a few weeks before. It was bittersweet every time I left him. Of
course I missed him. And he knew that. But it also felt good to be alone.
Being alone let me be close to Hana. It gave space for her story to breathe.

The day before I would go to Sine's home for my month-long stay, I
sat alone in a vegetarian restaurant in Freetown Christiania, a Copenhagen
neighborhood known for its anarchist roots and pot-friendly culture. It was
Valentine's Day 2015, and I was happily eating a big bowl of homemade
creole curry soup and a hearty piece of rye bread. Next to me was a couple
I assumed to be on a first date. He was British, and she American—or

Canadian. (I couldn't quite tell from her accent.) I eavesdropped, listening in on their conversation; they were talking about their grandparents. I smiled to myself and thought, That's what has brought me to Denmark.

After finishing my meal, I walked across the street to a café, ordered myself a chai tea, and opened my journal. The room was big and smokey. The sounds of muffled conversation in different languages surrounded me. After a few scribbled observations, I connected to Wi-Fi, and a number of messages flooded my phone. Friends from the States were checking to see if I was okay. There had been a shooting in Copenhagen. It was being reported as a terrorist attack.

I've been through this before, I thought to myself, comfortably numb as I finished my tea and closed my journal. The Boston Marathon bombings replayed in my head. I left the café and took the bus back across the city to where I was staying, listening to police cars pass me by.

I barely slept that night as my anxieties chased me in bed. To calm my mind, I counted in Polish, as Sergiusz had taught me to do. Then I tried to count how many modes of transportation I had been on since arriving in Europe. When that didn't work, I scrolled through my phone, looking at pictures of rustic weddings and white dresses on Pinterest. I watched shadows dance on the ceiling. I turned from one side to the other, then from my back to my stomach. The helicopters above told me that the manhunt was still underway. Every prolonged silence made me think that maybe the gunman had been found, but also made me wonder if perhaps the shadows belonged to him. (The police would catch him eventually, but not before he killed a volunteer guard at Copenhagen's main synagogue. In the hours I lay awake worrying, someone had died because he was a Jew.)

The next morning on the train, I squeezed my backpacks between my legs and watched as police officers and soldiers patrolled the platform. There was an eerie, uncomfortable silence, as if everyone was a suspect. Even so, no one asked me for an ID or my passport. I couldn't stop thinking about my grandmother running for her life because of who she was, while I was privileged enough to be ignored.

The train lurched forward. I stared out the window as we traveled south into the countryside. It was flat as far as I could see. Farmhouses blurred into a long line of wood and white paint. The fields blurred into a long line of dull brown ground and solid gray sky. The landscape soothed my anxiety.

Sine instructed me to get off the train in a town called Vordingborg. She told me it would be about twenty minutes from Næstved, where I had met Jensine. I listened to other passengers talk while catching glimpses of their reflections in the window and jotted down memories of my grandmother's stories in my phone. "Danish is a throat disease," she jokingly said to me on a few occasions. "Half the words are being swallowed." In my head I practiced my destination's name, swallowing the syllables.

Knud-Arne picked me up at the station, and we exchanged pleasantries while he drove. It had been a year and a half since I last saw him, and in that time his mother had passed away—now both Jensine and Hana were spoken about in the past tense. We drove by houses I had seen from the train. Their straw roofs and wood-trimmed windowpanes were reminiscent of drawings in fairytales. The farmland had rows of plants and harvested wheat. Each stalk of life was its own entity, waiting for the winter months to end. The names of the towns and the streets—Ørslev, Øster Egesborg, Mern, Tolstrupvej—appeared as random combinations of letters. "Sine and her family really live in the middle of nowhere," Knud-Arne warned me.

At a white church, we took a right. The road was hilly for Denmark. We came upon the small school Sine's children attended and made a left. A couple of houses speckled the neighborhood. One flagpole had a raised Danish flag; Knud-Arne said the flag was only raised to honor special occasions such as birthdays or weddings. We came to a barn with two small cows and a couple of horses grazing nearby. Knud-Arne pulled into the driveway as the sun was beginning to set. My grandmother's words and photographs passed through my head like a flip-book of memories, waiting to stop on this one.

Sine opened the door with a warm smile as her nine-year-old son ran up to us, his head just at his mother's waist. He extended his hand and said, "My name is Lauge," in well-practiced English.

"Nice to meet you, Lauge," I said, shaking his hand. "I'm Rachael." I gave Sine a hug, saying, "Thank you for having me."

Sine invited us into the house. I took off my winter boots and let my wool socks graze the cool kitchen floor. She placed a fresh pot of coffee on the table and encouraged us to sit. There was no special ritual. It simply felt like I had walked into the flow of her Sunday afternoon.

For the next few hours, we sat around the table drinking coffee and talking. "My grandmother was a happy person. We are a lot of children and grandchildren after her." Sine said to me. "Jensine used to get us all together every year at Christmas. She really cared about connecting people. That was a big thing for her. She always loved watching all of her children and grandchildren having a good time. And I had always heard the story about Hana. I just knew that she was a Jewish refugee who came, and my grandparents took care of her, and she was helping them on the farm. And of course my grandmom was very worried about Hana because she didn't know what happened after she left. So she was always thinking about, oh, what happened to her, and we never knew. Jensine really had been thinking a lot about it because it was a hard story about her. It was really not an everyday thing."

Sine had just turned forty and lived with her husband, Torsten, and their three kids—Liva, Lauge, and Silje. She told me I would live in one of their recently renovated apartments across the street. In the mornings I would help in the barn, and in the evenings I would cook dinner for the family. I had the afternoons to myself to read, write, photograph—whatever I wanted. Sine's life was of course different from Jensine's. I knew that. But being with her family made me feel like I was doing exactly what I had set out to do in following my grandmother's story.

Sine and I bonded quickly. In the mornings, as I scooped poop in the barn and cleaned the stalls, we would gossip about our families, sharing anecdotes about different people we were related to. And in the afternoons, as we drank coffee and ate rye bread (*rugbrød*) with cheese, we had lofty talks about politics and global warming and discussed plans for the future. Sergiusz and my recent engagement was a regular topic of conversation as well.

When we talked about following in our grandmother's footsteps, Sine told me, "My grandmother was a farm wife, I guess. I don't know what it is called, but her husband, Arne, was a farmer. And back then it was very normal that the lady was taking care of the children and helping with animals and in the field also, so she grew her own vegetables and had a big garden."

Before Sine and Torsten moved to the countryside, they were twenty-somethings living in Copenhagen. Sine was working as a physical therapist, but didn't cope well with the nine-to-five office life. So when the opportunity came for them to buy her uncle's farmhouse, they took it. "And you know, we had this space and started growing things," she said. "And we started getting sheep. And I had a horse. And chickens. And then it just grew, and soon we had three kids, and I found, oh, this is what I want to do. I think it is in my genes. It's in my blood or something."

"Do you mind raising animals for meat?" I asked her. My vegetarianism was also often discussed.

"I always said that if I get too used to death on a farm, I am not supposed to be a farmer anymore," she told me. "I still cry sometimes when I load the sheep, and even if it is just three roosters I have to take away, I will take them and give them a little kiss and say, 'I'm sorry, but you can't stay here.'"

I photographed everything I did on the farm. Each activity was symbolic, some reminder of words my grandmother had once written home to her parents:

> In Gørløse I learned how to work and I learned knitting. In Sonder-gaarden I learned how to work with chickens and hens. At Larsen's farm I learned how to cook and how to be independent. Now, in this place I am a completely independent worker; I can cook; I can take care of the children, which I really like. I am happy, really, trust me Mommy.

On Tuesday afternoons, I would join Sine and Liva in the barn, as was their mother-daughter routine. I photographed eleven-year-old Liva gently groom her seventeen-year-old pony named Ringo. I watched as she cleaned his hoofs and braided his mane, adding a little bit of glitter to his thick hair as a final touch.

> I prefer physical work to psychological [work]. If I work physically, I

can immediately see what I did: I baked this bread, I did this work in the garden.

I found as much comfort in my evening routine in the kitchen as I did with my morning routine in the barn. I watched the kids play outside while I cooked dinner and took breaks to jump with them on the trampoline.

But of course, I want to continue my education . . . It is not only that I want to know more and more, as Mommy wrote to me, but it is also for another reason: a clever person needs education, the basic education.

I photographed Sine when she fed the pigs, and I tagged along with her when she went to the slaughterhouse.

Jensine gives me such responsibility for work . . . They respect me.

I met many of Jensine's other descendants as well. She had five children and fifteen grandchildren. They all knew who I was.

With this new place I became new Hanka. I decided to fight for life, to be stronger. I am not as unhappy as before, for so many months. Now I am completely different: happy, full of life. I love all, I salute all people that I meet, I smile at them.

Everyone in the family heard the stories about Hana and reminded me of what Knud-Arne had first told me—this was a good story in their family. They helped save someone.

My Dear Daddy . . . You cannot imagine how important is a place where people live, how much influence it gives, how it is transforming. Here I am walking every day and singing, and I do not miss anything. Of course it is not perfect, but when I came here I felt like "home" . . . so trustful and open. I don't have any other word than "home."

I was responsible for preparing dinner, and on Wednesdays the kids helped. Liva went with me to the grocery store, and on our way she practiced her English and I practiced my Danish.

"School good?" I'd ask, giving her a thumb's up.

"Yes, yes," she'd reply shyly.

"Friends good?"

"Yes, yes."

Liva taught me the words for cheese (*ost*), bread (*brød*), and various vegetables—*tomat, agurk, løg*—making our way through Sine's grocery list.

I went to school with Liva and Lauge on a few occasions. I assisted with English lessons. The students asked me about my high school, what music I liked, if I had a boyfriend, and if I liked traveling. They also asked if I had heard about the Danish terror attack and if I had ever seen a school shooting. In a ninth-grade class that had just finished a unit on American history, the students asked me about racial prejudice and whether black people in America were treated differently than black people in Denmark.

Most of all, the students were curious why I was in Denmark. I tried to explain that Liva and Lauge's great-grandmother had taken care of my grandmother during World War II. One of Lauge's classmates, a third grader, asked why my grandmother had to leave Czechoslovakia, so I tried to explain that it was because the world was really scary then, especially if you were a Jew. Another student quickly raised his hand and asked, "What's a Jew?"

On most evenings, Sine, Torsten, and the kids sat in the living room while I cooked, which freed Sine from some of her usual family tasks. When they wandered into the kitchen, they'd tell me how good the food smelled. When it was ready, I'd cautiously tell them it was "*tid til mad*" (time for dinner). Over dinner, we sat around the table together discussing the events of the day. Silje, the littlest member of the family, always shared her seat with their elderly black cat. I loved being an integral part of their family time. It was so different from anything in my own life. For Sine's family, this dynamic was new as well. They had never had a stranger stay in their house for so long and in such an intimate way.

The darkness and silence that surrounded me in the Danish country-side became comforting throughout my time on the farm. I loved watching the sun set for miles and miles into the distance. I began to expect the harsh hit of the wind in the middle of the night and the hiss of the air that escaped from outside and into my apartment. The simplicity of the landscape calmed me. I had never felt anything like it. It was a daily life that felt intentional, manageable, and purposeful. Here, in what could be perceived as the middle of nowhere, I felt like I was somewhere.

CHAPTER 6

WHEN THE NAZIS CAME

The family's children taught me Danish and fooled me completely by teaching me the curse words. Instead of saying "thank you," I would walk around saying "fuck yourself." But you learn.

—HANA DUBOVÁ, 1998

The first time Hana said no to an adult was during her first year in Denmark. "One day there was a whole troop of Germans marching towards the farm, which was surrounded by fields," she began to tell me. "I saw German soldiers in German uniforms, and I thought they were coming for me—this is 1940—so I ran and hid in the outhouse. The soldiers wanted to buy supplies—feed for the horses and food for themselves. The farmer knew that I spoke German and came looking for me and asked me to negotiate with them. I am almost fifteen, and I had never said no to an adult—not to my parents or teachers. It would never even have occurred to me to say no. But I did say no to the farmer. The Germans stayed on the farm until they got what they wanted, and they paid extremely well for it. I was scared to leave the outhouse; I thought the farmer would throw me out, that I would land somewhere in the field and have nowhere to sleep and nothing to eat because for the first time in my life I said no to an adult, but eventually when I did come out, everything was fine."

When I went out to follow my grandmother's war story, I was deeply aware that unlike so many survivors, she never witnessed a murder. She was barely even asked about her Jewishness. While others were hiding in sewers and attics, she walked free in Denmark. While relatives were stuffed inside cattle cars and treated as if they were unworthy of life, Hana made her own decisions. While children witnessed their fathers disappear, or their mothers dragged by their hair from their homes, Hana was spared from such sights. While young mothers watched their newborns being thrown into piles of snow or smashed against brick walls by men ordered to hate, Hana thought about what it would be like to have a child of her own. When the Nazis came for her parents in Czechoslovakia, their neighbors turned a blind eye. But when the Nazis came for Hana in Denmark, her neighbors saved her.

In December 1941, the Japanese bombed Pearl Harbor, America joined the war, and Hana's daydream of being a pioneer in Palestine was pushed far away. The world was consumed with killing; travel routes were blocked and immigration, illegal and otherwise, stalled. More and more people from countries around the world were becoming displaced, but there was nowhere for them to go. Accepting that she would remain in Denmark, Hana began to yearn for days filled with learning rather than labor.

Education had always been put on a pedestal in her family. Books were always given for birthdays and holidays. And when the Nazis took away schooling from the Jews, parents and teachers met clandestinely in each other's homes to teach the children. "It was the most intensive learning," my grandmother told me. "As we said to each other, 'We will show them they cannot take education away from us.'"

In 1942 Hana began writing to schools to ask if in exchange for work scrubbing toilets or cleaning classrooms she could be a student. One school said yes. It was a finishing school in Sorø that taught young women about childcare, personal hygiene, folding napkins, and cooking, as well as Danish history, math, and geography. The irony was not lost on Hana that she would be the maid in a school where women were taught how to manage maids.

She arrived in the middle of the semester and was welcomed by the headmistress, who was dressed in black and wore a black bowler hat with a velvet black ribbon tied beneath her chin. "I was the true Cinderella," my grandmother said. "I was positively convinced that the other girls hated me. They were from well-to-do families. They all knew the right society, and I had nothing. I didn't even sleep in the dorms with the girls; they put me in the maid's quarters. I didn't belong there."

Every morning, Hana woke up and did her chores with the expectation that she would be in class by 8:30. She was filled with both appreciation and envy whenever she was around the other girls and was embarrassed by her thick accent. Her classmates were from the upper class. They had nice clothes and went to dances with boys. Hana had only one used uniform to wear, which had been given to her by the headmistress. She washed it every second day by hand and let it dry on the radiator overnight so it could be ironed the next morning.

In her room in the servants' quarters, she was given a bed, a desk, a chair, and a wardrobe. At night she would sit by a slanted window and diligently copy notes from a borrowed textbook into her notebook, always writing with a green pen. One night heavy snow came through her window, and all of the notes she had copied so carefully, word for word, became a puddle of green ink. "The world is falling apart around me," my grandmother said, reflecting back. "The letters from home had stopped coming. I was well aware of the German occupation in Denmark and grateful for how lucky I was being in school. My parents are in a concentration camp. And yet, in spite of it all I cried and cried over my washed-out handwritten notes, which I wrote so painstakingly between my chores. But it's so important what is in your head," she continued. "Like I said, I thought these girls hated me. On the farm, I was part of the family. At Christmas I went to church with them. I sat at dinner with them. I celebrated birthdays with them. I went to their grandparents with them. Now, at Christmas I had nowhere to go. So I asked the headmistress if I could stay at the school if I baked her cookies and emptied her chamber pot, and she agreed. Before Christmas came, we had this big holiday party with a gift exchange. I was cleaning the bathroom at the time because I didn't dare go to the party. But a classmate came and found me and asked me to join the group. And as a Christmas gift, all of the girls got together and gave me a uniform and a textbook and a small silver ring. So maybe they didn't hate me. Maybe they just felt sorry for me. To this day, it is the most precious gift I have ever received."

———————————

During the early years of the war, German soldiers nicknamed Denmark "the whipped-cream front" as it was a lovely place to be stationed. While their compatriots were facing bullets on the Eastern Front, the Germans stationed in Denmark were enjoying Danish pastries. To be in Denmark meant you were safe and in a place where there was plenty to eat. There were blond girls to date and beaches to enjoy. There was an air of normalcy and privilege there during an otherwise incredibly violent time.

Hitler saw Denmark as a natural ally. Even after the Wannsee Conference in January 1942, when fifteen high-ranking Nazi party and German government officials came together to discuss the implementation of the "Final Solution," the plan to systematically annihilate the Jews of Europe, Denmark was excluded. The Nazis assumed that they could get rid of the Danish Jews after they conquered the rest of Europe.

Life in Denmark remained relatively calm for much of the war. Both the occupied and the occupiers had an understanding of how Danish society should operate under Nazi rule. The Danes continued to supply the Germans with food, and the Germans left the Danes alone. The soldiers and German officials knew that if they targeted anyone living in Denmark, the situation would change. The Danish government remained steadfast in treating Jews in the same manner as everyone else.

In September 1942 Hitler sent the Danish king a lengthy telegram in honor of his seventy-second birthday. King Christian X responded with a rather impersonal note of appreciation, something along the lines of "Thank you very much for your congratulations." Hitler was enraged by the indifference toward him and political turmoil began to come to a boil in the model protectorate. Hitler appointed a Gestapo officer named Dr. Werner Best to subjugate the Danes that November. Best had spent years moving up the Nazi ranks. He had served as the Gestapo's legal adviser and was deputy to both Reinhard Heydrich and Heinrich Himmler, two of the most notorious Nazis. During the first half of the war, Best had been involved in the mass murder of Polish Jews and intellectuals as well as the persecution of Jews in Nazi-occupied France. As Denmark's new plenipotentiary, Best had full power to act on behalf of Germany.

Best had been warned by his predecessor that any action taken against the Jews would disrupt the continued cooperation of the Danes. He had nothing against persecuting the Jews—far from it—but he was pragmatic. Best understood that it was in his own self-interest to keep law and order in Denmark. If that meant not yet deporting the Danish Jews, he would make that compromise.

Around the time of Best's appointment, Hana graduated from finishing school and began working as a maid for a banker's family back in Næstved, not far from where she had lived with Jensine and Arne. "It was nothing like the farm," she told me. "I certainly was a maid. I couldn't eat with them. I couldn't use the same toilet they did. And I lived in a little room which was assigned to the maid. I was not a part of that family at all."

February 1943 brought a psychological turning point in the war. For close to four months, German forces had been fighting the Soviet Union for control of Stalingrad in southern Russia. To this day, it is considered one of the bloodiest battles in modern warfare. Nearly two million people were injured or killed. It was a massive loss for Germany, which was forced to surrender and relocate many of its soldiers who had been stationed in the west. The Soviet Union, an ally of Great Britain and the United States, was now taking control of the war.

This didn't stop the mass murder of the Jews. A harrowing fact is that when the "Final Solution" was planned at the Wannsee Conference, 80 percent of the Jews who would die in the Holocaust were still alive. Less than a year and a half later, the ratio was reversed. Four out of five Jews had been killed, but it would be years before anyone would know or be able to comprehend this statistic.

With the death toll rising across the globe and more and more nations involved in warfare, resistance movements and uprisings against the Nazi regime became more frequent. And very often, these were led by young people not much older than Hana. There were Sophie and Hans Scholl, former members of the Hitler Youth, who were beheaded by the Nazis in 1943 for distributing leaflets with anti-Nazi sentiments. They were both in their early twenties. And there were the young Jewish partisans who engaged in guerrilla warfare and acts of sabotage against the Nazi occupation. There were acts of resistance in the ghettos—both physical and spiritual. In the Warsaw Ghetto, the most notorious of the ghettos created by the Nazis, the Oneg Shabbat Archive was established by Emanuel Ringelblum. In an environment where writing your own story could get you killed, Ringelblum and a group of writers, thinkers, and artists of all ages risked their lives to document life as it was in the ghetto. So much of what we know now is thanks to them. Then in April 1943, when the Warsaw Ghetto Uprising began, it was led by young people, almost all of whom had lost their entire families to Nazi brutality. It took the Germans nearly a month to suppress it. They lit buildings on fire, turning the ghetto into a death trap and burning thousands of people alive. By the end of the uprising, the Nazis had killed fourteen thousand Jews and sent another forty thousand to the camps. Then they razed the notorious Warsaw Ghetto to the ground. A similar uprising occurred in Sobibor extermination camp as well. That is where my family was murdered. Hana's parents' and brother's ashes laid the foundation for the revolt.

From the east to the west, Allied and Axis powers were killing each other with speed, escalating the violence that would lead to the end of the war. Neutrality was no longer an option. The whole world was taking sides.

In Denmark, things were changing as well. Nourished by civic solidarity, the underground Danish resistance movements grew stronger and increased their anti-German sabotage. Then on August 29, 1943, the Germans officially dissolved the Danish government and instituted martial law. At this time, prominent leaders throughout Denmark were arrested, and a plan to deport the Danish Jews was put in place. King Christian X stopped riding through the city and declared himself a Nazi prisoner of war in his own country. The time of the "whipped-cream front" had come to an end.

When the Nazis officially dissolved the Danish government, Werner

Best informed his confidant, German diplomat Georg Duckwitz, that the roundup of the Danish Jews would happen on October 1, 1943—on the Jewish New Year. Duckwitz, who was serving as an attaché for Nazi Germany, knew the Danish community intimately. He had first moved to Copenhagen in 1928 and had been taken with certain aspects of Scandinavian socialism that he found similar to the nationalistic ideology of the Nazi Party that was just starting to gain popularity in Germany. After Hitler was elected in 1933, Duckwitz accepted a position in Berlin with the Office of Foreign Affairs, but he quickly became disillusioned by the party's politics and in 1935 stepped down from his role, stating, "I am so fundamentally deceived in the nature and purpose of the National Socialist movement that I am no longer able to work within this movement as an honest person." In 1939 he was assigned by the Third Reich to the German Embassy in Copenhagen as a maritime attaché.

When Duckwitz learned about the plans to deport Denmark's Jews, he traveled to Berlin to try to stop it through official channels. When that didn't work, he flew to Stockholm, ostensibly to discuss the passage of German merchant ships through Swedish waters. But while he was there, he contacted the Swedish prime minister, Per Albin Hansson, to ask if Sweden would accept Jewish refugees from Denmark. Hansson agreed.

Back in Denmark, Duckwitz contacted a Danish politician named Hans Hedtoft to let him know about the planned deportation. Hedtoft then warned the head of the Jewish community. The chief rabbi had been arrested when martial law was declared in Denmark, so the warning came to the acting chief rabbi, Marcus Melchior. What happened next was a spontaneous act of humanity.

On September 29, 1943, as the Jewish community gathered in the Great Synagogue in Copenhagen to welcome the Jewish New Year, Rabbi Melchior prepared his remarks. I imagine him like a biblical prophet standing on the bimah and speaking to a distressed crowd. He warned his fellow Jews. He told them to go home and pack their belongings. He said that Denmark was no longer safe and that it was time to flee. "You must also speak to your Christian friends and ask them to warn any Jews they know. You must do this immediately, within the next few minutes, so that two or three hours from now everyone will know what is happening. By nightfall we must all be in hiding."

Jews found refuge with Christian friends in the city and the countryside, with neighbors and employers. When Gestapo officers arrived at the homes of Jews, they found themselves pounding their fists into silence. Apartments and houses were empty; the Jews were being hidden in summer homes, basements, and on farms. Many were taken to Copenhagen's Bispebjerg Hospital, where they were checked in as patients under typical Danish names—Jensen, Nielsen, Christiansen, Johansen. Psychiatric wards and nurses' quarters were filled with the threatened neighbors. The entire medical staff, and most countrymen and countrywomen, cooperated to save Jewish lives. They promised to protect their belongings, water their plants, and take care of their property. It was no secret that the Nazis violently retaliated against those who helped the Jews and not uncommon for entire communities to be eradicated if they resisted. But in Denmark, the protection of the Jews had become a symbol of Danish autonomy, and almost everyone did his or her part, no matter how dangerous. During these weeks, even staying silent about the improvised rescue was a form of resistance.

Rabbi Marcus Melchior, his pregnant wife, and their four children hid in a priest's home for ten days as thousands of Jews were smuggled to Sweden on illegal fishing boats. The Danish fishermen mostly left from northern Denmark as it was only an hour from the Swedish coast. When it came time for Rabbi Melchior and his family to make the crossing, they were directed to travel south by train to a bishop's home in a city called Nykøbing Falster. There had been a recent raid on a church in the north where Jews were hiding, and seventy-five people were deported to the Theresienstadt concentration camp. It was no longer safe to flee from there.

On the train ride, the rabbi's wife, Meta, and their youngest son sat in first class to avoid any questioning, unsure if the five-year-old would be able to stay quiet. The rest of the family sat in coach. Bent, their fourteen-year-old son, watched passengers read German newspapers and stared at the German soldiers who patrolled the train. He clutched what he carried with him closely—a few pairs of underwear and a book of mathematical problems. Every stranger felt like a potential threat.

The family arrived at the bishop's home late that afternoon and was told that many others were hiding in the nearby church. Then the bishop, knowing that Marcus was a rabbi, asked if there was anything he could do, any meal he could make, to help them observe the holiday. It was October 8, the first night of Yom Kippur.

Hana hadn't known anything about the raid against the Jews until a member of the Danish resistance showed up at the banker's house in Næstved. "One day a young man I had never seen before nor after came for me," she told me. "He asked the banker, 'Do you have a Jewish servant here?' He then told them that there would be a raid against the Jews and he was here to escort me to safety. So, then he came to me and asked, 'Do you have a bike?' I said yes. He said, 'Get on the bike and follow me.' Today, if my children or grandchildren followed someone on a bike, I would kill them. But it was a different world."

Like the obedient child she had always been, Hana did what she was told. She collected a few of her belongings, got on her bike, and peddled as fast as she could to keep up with the stranger who had come for her. She never asked him who he was or where he came from or where she was going. In her story, he was nameless and faceless.

He led her to a tall white church that sat like a crown worn by the dark-blue sky. The shadow of the pastor appeared in the doorway and led her to the bell tower, where about a dozen people already sat waiting. It was dark and cold within the walls built from raw wood. A few small round windows offered just enough natural light to remind one that day always becomes night.

Food was brought to them a couple of times a day, but Hana never ate. She slept on a straw mattress as she had been trained to do at summer camp. And every hour, on the hour, she covered her ears when the church bell was rung by hand.

On the third night in the church, a signal came. It was time to go. Hana quickly went down the narrow stairs, past the sanctuary's balcony and pews, and into the autumn night. She ran toward the shore and hid underneath an upside-down rowboat in the sand. During the occupation, her body had developed from girlhood to womanhood, and her clothes were ill-fitting; safety pins struggled to keep her blouse from opening.

Her breath grew more erratic when the next signal came. She ran toward the edge of the water. In her head she kept repeating to herself, *He isn't going to take me. The fisherman isn't going to take me. I have no money. I have nothing. He isn't going to take me.*

She turned her pockets inside out as if to prove her lack and, in her accented Danish, whispered to the silhouette of her rescuer, *"Jeg har ingen penge"* (I have no money).

He looked her in the eyes and said, "I didn't ask you, did I? Hop on board."

Marcus, Meta, Bent, and the other Melchior children boarded the boat and handed the fisherman a hefty sum of money, far more than what a rabbi's salary could afford. The other passengers, including Hana, were strangers who had been hiding throughout the town. There were nineteen people altogether. The fisherman instructed everyone to lie down so he could cover them with a linen-like tarp and a slew of freshly caught herring. The refugees lay silently as their hero worked quickly.

Then the fisherman undocked the boat.

Anxious breaths filled the air.

It was past 7:00 p.m. when the fisherman pulled away from the shore. The sky mirrored the depth of the sea, illuminated by more stars than usual, as though the spirits of those who had sent Hana to safety four years before had taken shape as lambent guardians of the night. The refugees lay silent, unsure of where they were going or what they were running from. Plans for the days and the years ahead dissolved, pushed further away with each wave that washed against their overcrowded boat.

The season of early sunrises was over, so they should have had enough time to make it to Sweden in the dark. The passengers understood that there were few possibilities—either they would make it to Sweden or be caught by the Nazis. The only other option was to drown. Hana carried with her a small vial of poison that her father had given her when she left Czechoslovakia. Marcus and Meta also had a plan—if the Nazis were to capture them, they would take a child under each of their arms and jump into the sea.

"We were caught by the German patrol," my grandmother told me. She remembered hearing heavy boots on the deck and German voices telling the fisherman to immediately sail back to Denmark. "They stopped the boat. We could hear them walking on top of the fish . . . and I tell you, to this day I believe they knew we were there. They couldn't have not known. Maybe I am crazy, but they never uncovered the fish. They never took a shovel to see if something was under the fish. I think that they were young guys who were just tired of this whole thing. I mean, I interpret it because otherwise it is impossible they would not see what is in the boat."

So the fisherman sailed on.

When day broke, no land was in sight and the Danes panicked. The sun was rising in the wrong direction, and they were running low on fuel. Everyone knew that they should have arrived in Sweden by now. Many of the passengers became seasick. Hana helped empty buckets of vomit over the side of the boat as rumors started to spread. Some declared the fisherman to be a criminal, claiming he was only making the crossing for profit. Others thought he might be a drunk. But everyone understood that, regardless of the reason, he didn't know where they were. He finally admitted that he had never sailed into open waters before and didn't know how to use his compass. He was lost and scared.

It would be many hours before a shoreline appeared in the distance. No one knew what country they saw, but knew that only Sweden was safe. Every other country, including a return to Denmark, would have brought danger if not immediate death. The refugees stared blankly into the gray, damp afternoon.

Fog coated the coast where a six-year-old boy named Per-Arne Persson happily kicked a soccer ball around across from his family's home. It was October 9, 1943, and it was his birthday.

Even the youngest of children knew that war surrounded them. It was common to see blackout curtains over windows or hear fighter planes overhead. So when young Per-Arne noticed a strange boat idling in the sea, he abandoned his game and ran inside to tell his father.

Together with his neighbor, Per-Arne's father took their rowboat to investigate. As they neared the boat, the outlines of more and more people emerged from the fog—their exhausted faces pale and struck with fear, desperate for warmth and safety. Some refused to emerge from underneath the herring, terrified of who they were about to encounter.

Per-Arne's father looked toward the panicked fisherman and the frightened passengers and said, "Welcome to Sweden."

CHAPTER 7

YOU HAD TRUST IN PEOPLE

The world would be a sad place without progress if we didn't try to change the injustice we see and feel.

—HANA DUBOVÁ, 2005

There is an honorific from Yad Vashem, the Holocaust museum in Israel, called "Righteous among the Nations" that is given to non-Jewish individuals who saved Jews during the war. Perhaps the most well-known of the recipients is Oskar Schindler, who saved more than a thousand Jews from being deported to Auschwitz by giving them jobs in his factory. Or Raoul Wallenberg, a diplomat from Sweden, who saved tens of thousands of Jews in Hungary by providing them with certificates of protection. There are also lesser-known recipients, like Martha and Waitstill Sharp from Massachusetts, who, as Unitarian aid workers, sailed to Europe in 1939 to help relocate thousands of refugees. The only country as a whole to receive this honor is Denmark.

Denmark saved nearly 95 percent of its Jewish population. In little more than three weeks, more than seven thousand people (including non-Jewish spouses and prominent members of the underground) illegally sailed across the Baltic Sea to Sweden, whose government promised immediate and unconditional sanctuary for all those fleeing Denmark. Fewer than five hundred Jews were caught by the Nazis during this rescue operation and deported to Theresienstadt.

"Had it not been for the Danes, who knows where I would be," my grandmother once said. "The Danes said that anybody who lives on Danish soil, regardless who he is—Jew, non-Jew, citizen, noncitizen—is going to be treated like a Dane and not like anybody else." She wanted me and everyone who knew her story to understand that collective community is not only responsible for committing wrongdoing but also for saving lives.

When my grandmother died, I thought I had lost the chance to ask questions about her history to people who were there. Hearing about her experiences was contagious. I loved observing the silences when she spoke; the moments when she would search for the words that became the signposts of her stories. Sometimes she would keep straight on with the story, and sometimes she would go off on a tangent. She listed her unsung heroes not by their names or faces but by what they did. "It was a different world," she told me. "You had trust in people." Her memories were an adventure. Each retelling was honest. Each retelling was unique.

She told me about the Melchior family—the famous rabbi and his family who were on the same boat she was. Her memory of Marcus Melchior, a man who had become a symbol of the rescue within this chapter of history, was coated in resentment, however. She was angry, even as she retold the story many decades later, that he didn't help her upon her arrival in Sweden.

The Melchior family name became well-known after the Holocaust. When the war ended, Marcus returned to Denmark and became the chief rabbi of the country. His son Bent would follow in his footsteps. Bent's son Michael would go on to become the chief rabbi of Norway and a member of Israel's Knesset. And Michael's son Jair, who was raised in Israel, would return to his father's homeland of Denmark and become the chief rabbi there as well.

When I came to Denmark in 2015, I reached out to the Jewish community and told them about my connection to this seemingly dynastic family. And that is how I was introduced to Bent. Just a few days before I moved to the farm and met Sine, I made my way to Bent's home. I remember walking up the flights of stairs to his apartment in Copenhagen feeling nervous and excited, as though I were unknotting another thread of my grandmother's story.

When Bent opened the door, I saw an elderly man with a slight hunch-back. He wore a pressed white shirt, black pants, and a black kippah on his head. At eighty-five years old, he still lived independently. Every day, he visited his wife of over sixty years in a nearby nursing home.

He gave me a warm hug and invited me to sit on the couch. He sat down on a red chair across from me. After some cordial small talk, I asked if I could record the conversation. "Sure, sure," he said. I pressed record on a small handheld unit and placed my camera next to it on the table. My impression was that he simply thought I was an American journalist coming to learn about the rescue. His was an outspoken voice not just for the memory of this history but for refugees' rights throughout the world—from Denmark to the Soviet Union to Bosnia and South Africa. He was used to people wanting to hear his story.

"I have tried, in my life, to serve the community," he told me matter-of-factly. "I was a teacher. I am a rabbi. I was chief rabbi of Denmark. I worked for many organizations, among them the Danish Refugee Council. I have translated parts of the Bible into Danish and parts of the Jewish prayer book into Danish. I have written my memoirs when I thought I was at the end of my life, but now that is almost twenty years ago. So I still look ahead."

I told him where I was from, what my parents did, and about my recent engagement. I explained to him what I was trying to do by following my grandmother's story, adding a bold claim at the end. "She was on the same boat as you," I said. "When you fled Denmark in 1943."

He looked at me thoughtfully. "Were there any other relatives of hers from Czechoslovakia who survived?"

I told him of a few distant family members—a cousin, an uncle, and a couple of aunts whose survival was due to their interfaith marriages. "It's no reason to marry someone, but it certainly makes a case for interfaith marriage," I added with a slight lift in my voice.

"To think of a girl of fourteen," he pondered out loud. "To think of the parents who sent away their little girl to a strange country. I mean, the parents must have been desperate. And then the fact that we, with differ-ent backgrounds—she was already a refugee, and we were not refugees until we came on board the boat—had the same chances to survive or to go down in the sea."

We began to exchange details of the story. A lot of it matched up, like how many people were on board and how many extra hours it took to get to Sweden. "We were one of the last boats to leave the country," he told me. "The Baltic Sea is not the biggest sea in the world. But we didn't have fuel." He continued, "In school, we were taught that the sun rises in the east and I knew that Sweden was in the east, but when the sun rose that morning at sea, we could see that we were sailing in the wrong direction. It was already dangerous enough to be sailing during the nighttime, but during the day we would be easy to spot. We thought that the fisherman was a traitor, but he was as afraid as we were. He had never been out in the sea without seeing land. He had never navigated. He had bought a compass, but he didn't know what to do with it."

Other memories didn't match up, like the story Hana told me about the German soldiers coming on board. I didn't tell him that my grandmother resented his father. It didn't seem necessary or relevant. I hadn't followed my grandmother's story to hold onto her pain.

"There are a number of factors for why the rescue operation worked," Bent pointed out. "The fact that we had Sweden nearby was important. Also, we were not wearing any yellow stars here. In other countries, the Nazis said you should stop doing business with Jews, and they put them in a ghetto, so they were already somehow isolated before they were brought to the concentration camps. Here in Denmark, it was one action, one deportation. So for the Danes, the Jewish people were normal citizens and good neighbors. That was psychologically an important part of the story. But what I am always saying is that this was not something that was organized by an institution or government. This was grassroots. It was a spontaneous reaction of the men and women in the streets. These were our neighbors. We have legends around what happened during the war, but these are not legends; these are real incidents."

Bent asked me what I would do with my reporting and where I would go after Denmark. When would I return to Boston? And who was my fiancé? Was he Jewish?

I bragged that although not Jewish, Sergiusz was fluent in Hebrew and that he knew more about Jewish history than most people. Then I shared the long story about how we had met in Israel and were just friends until I decided to move to Europe. "In a way my grandmother's story brought us together," I told him.

"For many, many years, I have been on the same line as official Judaism," he said in response, "that mixed marriages were poison. And whatever means you have to stop it, you should use. Rabbis have been banging on the pulpit for generations and shouting, 'There shouldn't be mixed marriages!' And I have been banging the pulpit too." He paused. "But when God gives you a long life, he gives you time to think. And at one point I thought, We have been using these tactics for—I will just say, 'the last hundred years,' but of course it is much longer—and to which results but an increasing number of mixed marriages? For God's sake, at some point you have to stop and say, Are my tactics good? And the fact is, no. You are getting young people to turn their back to Judaism instead of drawing them near."

Surrounding us were Bent's books, some of which he authored. There were photographs of his family, pieces of Judaica, framed honors and letters of recognition. He pointed out one of the letters and told me it had come to his father from King Christian X during World War II. "The occasion was that my father had sent him his book that he had written together with another rabbi. And the king sat down and wrote this letter. He took the opportunity to wish the Jewish community Happy New Year."

"What happened when you arrived in Sweden?" I asked, redirecting our conversation back to Hana's story. "My grandmother told me that the wives of the fishermen in this little town in Sweden were fighting over who would take who for lunch. She told me she followed your family into the home of one of the fishermen, and that they laid out a big spread for all of you—cheeses, herring, sausages, breads."

Bent confirmed that this was true, at least the food part. He didn't remember my grandmother, but enough of the details of that night matched up that it seemed plausible they were together. So, in this way we corroborated my grandmother's memories.

"You know, I am still in touch with this boy," he told me, referring to

Per-Arne. "Well, he isn't a boy anymore, but he was when he first saw our boat drifting on his sixth birthday in 1943. He lives in the same house he did when we were there after the rescue. It's just a hundred meters or so from the Baltic Sea."

———————

A few weeks later in Sweden, I looked down at the stones beneath my feet, grabbed a few, and rubbed their smooth edges like a good luck charm. I pocketed one, a perfectly round light-tan stone with barely any blemishes, and threw the others back into the sea. Bent's words were in my thoughts. "Stones can tell stories," he had said.

The water was quiet. The waves lapped against the sand with a peaceful rhythm. There was no urgency to scamper backward. Had my feet gotten wet, a warm home awaited me nearby. My jacket was zipped up, and my scarf was wrapped tightly around my neck.

"The weather was just like this," Annika, Per-Arne's daughter, told me. I was standing with her and her older sister, Monica. The sky was gray and the air a comforting cold. "That is what my father told me. He was playing football here when he saw the boat. It was about five hundred meters from the shore." She pointed from the land to the sea. "It took my grandfather four trips and nearly two hours to bring all of the refugees to shore."

Here I was, in a little Swedish village called Beddingestrand, standing in the exact spot where my grandmother's refugee boat had come to shore. Never in all my early years of research did I think I would find this place. I hadn't even thought to try. But when Bent told me that his family had stayed in touch with the fisherman's family, I knew I had to meet them. So I had emailed Annika and introduced myself, explaining that her grandfather had saved my grandmother during the rescue of the Danish Jews in 1943. She wrote me back quickly to let me know that she had translated my email for her parents, and they extended an invitation for me to visit their home.

I arrived on a Friday afternoon in late March. Outside the house was their family name, Persson, and a carefully mounted cast-iron ship. Playful windmills, random knickknacks, and some garden gnomes decorated the property. The most defining characteristic was a laundry line of small worn flags blowing in the wind. I looked at each of them, trying to name the countries in my head—Sweden, Denmark, Germany, Finland, Italy, Ireland, Ukraine, Israel, China, Poland, the United Kingdom, the United States. At the end was the light-blue flag of the United Nations. Its emblem of the world surrounded by two olive branches was adopted a year after the end of World War II. A line of faux imprint fossils of creatures from the past led me to their doorway. The salty air filled my nose.

Inside their home, I was greeted by a profusion of artifacts. There must have been two dozen clocks lining the dining room—digital clocks, antique clocks, clocks that made whimsical sounds on the hour. For a couple who was unable to leave the house without assistance, time was of the essence.

Photographs covered the walls of the living room. A guest book was set out on the coffee table waiting for me. "It is a big story in our family," Annika explained, repeating the same sentiment Sine had expressed when we got to talking about my grandmother. "When my grandfather went out to the boat and said to the refugees, 'Welcome to Sweden,' that was the biggest thing. Our history is always speaking about that."

Annika sat on the floor near me, with half of her face lit by the sun and the other half in shadow. She was in her forties and the younger daughter by eight years. "My father often talked about this history. Every day almost. Because we lived in my grandfather's house, it was always, 'My grandfather did this,' or, 'He did that,' or, 'This is what it was like when I was young.'"

Per-Arne, tall and lean, sat astute in his chair. He was now in his seventies, and his physical disabilities restricted his movements; he couldn't even walk to the shore anymore. He wore brightly colored rubber bracelets made by his granddaughter on his right wrist. On his fingers were several thick silver rings, and around his neck hung a chain with a golden trident and a photo of himself in the coast guard.

Marianne, his wife, sat in her wheelchair by his side. The two had met in a restaurant in Malmö in the mid-1960s and spent many of their fifty years together living in this house built by his grandfather in 1882.

I sat on the couch with my cameras next to me and my recorder going.

The entire family, including husbands and grandchildren, had come to meet me. The language barrier was stronger with the Perssons than with anyone I had met in Denmark. I relied on the combined English skills of the younger generation to translate Per-Arne's stories.

"Bent told me that your mother was Danish," I asked, looking at Per-Arne for confirmation before turning to Annika for a translation.

"Yes, she was Danish. I don't know how to say it, but my grandmother and my grandfather were very strong people," Annika responded. "They didn't like that there was a lot of people who didn't share their opinion about things during the war. The important thing for them was to welcome and to help people. Whatever, whoever it was. Of course, because she was Danish, my grandmother could talk to the people escaping Denmark and make it a bit calmer. It was a little bit of hysteria when they came with the boat because they didn't know where they were."

Per-Arne then continued in Swedish about how the military had surrounded his home because of his parents' involvement in getting the refugees to shore. "They stayed all night outside the house with guns, but my parents weren't scared." His voice was a deep and melodic soundtrack to the mental snapshots I was taking of their home. Nautical-themed relics covered all of the spare spaces—replicas of ships, small statues of navy men, a brass helm, formal and informal hats worn by soldiers at sea. I registered each piece as if taking inventory of their memories.

Annika's older sister, Monica, sat on a couch across from me with her husband and ten-year-old daughter, who was flipping through the pages of the family photo album. "She is very interested in history," they said. Above their heads hung a framed newspaper with the headline, KENDER I DEN OM RABBINEREN OG SILDEFISKEREN? (Do you know [the story] about the rabbi and the herring fisherman?) Annika explained, "It's from when Bent came to visit for the seventieth anniversary of the rescue. My mother wants to know, Did you hear this story when you were growing up?"

"It was the biggest of my grandmother's stories," I told them. "I thought it was like an action movie. Stuffed underneath herring. Lost at sea. Running from the Nazis. Does your father remember her?"

"He was so young. It is hard for him to remember," she said. "His older brother was sixteen at the time and remembers more, but it is too hard for him to talk about. He understood better what was going on at the time."

"I brought pictures," I then offered, pulling a small stack of photographs from my backpack. I moved from the couch, taking a seat on my knees between Marianne's and Per-Arne's chairs. "This is me and my grandmother," I told them, first showing a color photograph from a Passover seder. "I was about twenty then." I handed it to Marianne. "And this is my grandmother when she arrived at her first farm in 1939, so just a few years younger than when she came to your home." I handed this second photo, which was black and white and from my grandmother's archive, to Per-Arne. He examined it closely before speaking.

"He thinks he remembers her," Annika said. "He thinks she was the one helping clean the boat and was the last to get off."

More conversation continued around me in Swedish before Annika piped, "My mother says you look like your grandmother."

I looked at her and laughed, "People always tell me that, but it wasn't true when I was a kid."

Per-Arne replayed what he remembered from that night. He spoke confidently, having refined the story over the decades. He said that he ran to his father and told him that he had seen the boat and that his father and a neighbor went to investigate, concerned over whoever it was sailing so close to the shore. It took four trips to get all of the people to land. Each trip was fifteen minutes out and fifteen back, but sometimes it took longer because the Danes were too scared to leave the boat. He stated that there were other fishermen who wanted to help, but they didn't. He said that they were too afraid. Then he talked about the Melchior family staying over that night and how because Meta was pregnant, she got to sleep on the good couch even though it was normally forbidden to even put your feet up on it.

"One of the reasons that this history has stayed so present," Annika interjected, "is first, that my father is a really good storyteller, but also because the Melchior family stayed in touch with my grandparents. Every year on October 9, the anniversary of when they were rescued, they would write to my family."

Marianne moved herself to her desk in the corner of the crowded room, easily maneuvering her wheelchair between the coffee table and the other furniture. There were pieces of paper, printouts of emails, and random gifts all piled up on the desk. She pulled out an overstuffed white binder and handed it to me.

I began to flip through the plastic-covered pages that contained every written exchange between the Persson and Melchior families. The letters from Marcus were always addressed to *"Hr Per Persson och familj"* (Swedish for "Mr. Per Persson and family"). Bent's greetings often began with *"Kære venner!"* (Danish for "dear friends"). The international postage memorialized heroes from another era.

When I got to the end, I noticed my own name. It was my first email to them, printed and cataloged in the back. I stopped and pointed and smiled. "It's me!" I said looking up at Marianne. She had taken on the family story as her own. Like my grandmother, she organized everything so her grandchildren would know what happened that day in 1943. The clocks continued ticking, ushering in the passing days in a house where it felt like time had stood still.

"My father says it is not so strange that they remember, because it was nineteen people they saved," Annika said as she watched me flip through the pages of correspondence. "And he is wondering, If your grandmother came here by boat, where did she go after?"

CHAPTER 8

I NEVER STAYED PUT

Being alone, completely alone with myself—sometimes it is good, and sometimes it hurts and I want to run away, away from it all.

—HANA'S DIARY, 1941

Hana spent her first night in Sweden in a house that had formerly been used as a bed-and-breakfast. Annika and Monica took me to see this place; it was just a few blocks from their parents' home. On Hana's second day in Sweden, she and the other refugees were taken by the Swedish Red Cross to an agricultural high school in a nearby town called Åkarp. The students were on a break to help their families with the potato harvest, so the gymnasium and other facilities were used as a processing center for the newly arrived Danes. "I was asking everyone about my Czech friends. I was trying to find out whether the other *chaverim* got to Sweden," my grandmother told me. Hana was surrounded by hundreds of other people, but alone in figuring out how to survive on the periphery of war.

"The Red Cross gave us a medical examination and quarantined us. But before they quarantined us, they asked all these questions. 'Do you have relatives?' 'Do you have any way to make a living in Sweden?' And so on," she said. "I told them I didn't have anyone."

"What language were you speaking?" I asked her.

"Mostly Danish I think," she said. Danish and Swedish are kind of alike. "It was total immersion though, like on the farm. You had to figure it out. They also came with clothing for us," she continued. "They gave me black panties, a black bra, a black slip, and a black blouse. And I thought it was absolutely the sexiest thing I have ever seen in my life. Then they examined us and gave me a pill and told me to insert the pill in my vagina when I have sex. I was so insulted. I said, 'What do you think I am? Am I a prostitute or something like that? Am I a street girl? Am I a whore? First you give me black underwear, and now you give me this pill.' I really knew nothing about men. Now I understand that the pill was for pregnancy prevention. So I don't blame them for giving it to me."

I laughed. As long as I had known her, my grandmother was a proponent of sex appeal and femininity. She had a habit of hiking up my skirt and telling me to show off my legs. In her archive, I found pictures of her naked from a few years after this incident with the black lingerie. There is a whole series of her laying nude on a rock by the water. They were taken by a friend of hers. It is postwar boudoir photography. "That was my first impression of Sweden," she said. "My second impression of Sweden was when I walked on the streets and—for the first time in a long, long time— saw that there was not a blackout. In Prague there had been a blackout already since 1938. In other words, no streetlights and blacked-out windows in case we are bombed. In Denmark there was also a blackout all the time. And now, suddenly there are streetlights and they are playing *Gone with the Wind*, which had neon lights on the street. The Red Cross gave us tickets for the movie. It was my first Technicolor picture. Everything was black and white before."

Sweden had managed to stay neutral during World War II, as it had in World War I. But neutrality, like all positions during war, comes at a cost. In the first half of the war, some of Sweden's decisions benefited the German efforts, such as continuing trade. The Germans relied heavily on Sweden's natural resources—especially iron ore, which was a necessary mineral in the creation of steel, an important material for Germany's war efforts and their economy. And throughout 1940, Germany used Swedish railroads and coastal waters for the invasion of Norway. Although Sweden didn't know it when accepting this compromise of aiding the enemy in exchange for neutrality, keeping their rule was critical for their role in the rescue of the Danish Jews.

In a population of just over six million, there were about seven thousand Jews living in Sweden prior to the war, and most resided in Stockholm. And like many countries, neutral or not, Sweden limited immigration at the onset of World War II, even for temporary residency. Most Jews who sought refuge were refused, but as the war went on, Sweden's attitude changed, and it took in tens of thousands of their fellow Europeans. When the Nazis began to persecute the Jews of Norway in 1942, Sweden accepted nine hundred of them, over half of Norway's Jewish population. And in 1943, they agreed, thanks to Duckwitz's request, to take in the more than seven thousand Jews from Denmark—my grandmother included.

After being quarantined by the Swedish Red Cross and then processed, Hana, like every other Dane, had to figure out where to go. Having no one to help her, she asked the school if she could stay and work in the kitchen since the students were returning from the harvest season. "They gave me a job cleaning herring, and I got room and board. Imagine, after I was laying underneath the herring on the boat for all of those hours, now I was cleaning it every day. I wore a big heavy sack apron and also had to clean the huge vats that the oatmeal was cooked in. They were so big that I could step inside of them to clean them."

Hana stayed at the school for eight months and then began writing to nursing schools, thinking that she could do the same thing she did in Denmark—work in exchange for an education. "There weren't many options for women at this time," she told me. "I couldn't be a schoolteacher, because I had an accent and Swedish was not my first language. I had already been a maid. So I figured being a nurse was a good choice. And this would be a good profession if I went to Palestine. So I made the same deal. I would clean the toilets, corridors, and rooms for a free education. The school that accepted me was close to the Arctic Circle, way, way up north."

"Did you know about what was happening in the war?" I asked her. "Did you know where your parents and Petr were?"

"Like I said, the letters from home stopped coming around the time I went to the finishing school. We were slowly finding out about concentration camps, and I think I just understood that my family was gone. I really wanted to find the *chevrah* [her Czech friends]. I didn't know which of them made it to Sweden, but it wasn't so easy. We didn't have phone numbers."

Hana was eighteen now and popular with the other nursing students as she always wanted to work the weekend shifts. "I had nowhere to go," she said. "I envied them because I had no family life. I wandered around a lot. I never stayed put." Even on her own, Hana could live with the illusion of normalcy. When she buried her head in her schoolbooks and worked her twelve-hour shifts, she could pretend that there was no war.

Around this time, the Allied forces began a massive invasion of Europe. Over 150,000 British, Canadian, and American soldiers landed on the beaches of Normandy, France, in June 1944, forcing Hitler to relocate his army and his resources to Western Europe. This resulted in Germany's defeat in the East. With Hitler now distracted with fighting the Americans and the British, Soviet troops could advance into Poland, Czechoslovakia, Hungary, and Romania.

The Soviet Army's rapid advance surprised the Germans, and they rushed to destroy the evidence of their mass murder. This led to one of the first liquidations of a concentration camp—Majdanek—in July. The Germans demolished the camp built in occupied Poland. But the gas chambers remained standing.

The Nazis transported the prisoners deep into Germany to other concentration camps—some by train, but most in forced marches. The victims walked hundreds of miles without proper clothing or shoes. Tens of thousands of people died in these death marches from hunger or because they were shot when they couldn't keep up.

Among those who did survive, many ended up at Bergen-Belsen, a concentration camp in Germany. It was overcrowded and plagued with disease. In April 1945, when British soldiers liberated the camp, they found a scene unimaginable even for a horror movie. Thousands of dead bodies were strewn about the camp. There was no running water. The sixty thousand prisoners still alive were stuffed into barracks. They were fed only three times a week.

A British soldier who was a member of the Army Film and Photographic Unit recalled, "The bodies were a ghastly sight. Some were green.

They looked like skeletons covered with skin—the flesh had all gone. There were bodies of small children among the grown-ups. In other parts of the camp there were hundreds of bodies lying around, in many cases piled five or six high."

Two weeks later, after the liberation of Bergen-Belsen, Hitler killed himself in his underground bunker. A little more than a week after that, Germany surrendered. The war was over.

The statistics were staggering. Between the years of 1939 and 1945, more than fifty countries were involved and more than 70 million individuals were enlisted to fight in their nation's armed forces. From America, more than 16 million troops served. In Germany, more than 3.5 million soldiers were left dead, and there were 9 million civilian deaths in total. In the Soviet Union, the numbers of deceased military personnel surpassed 7.5 million, but counting the entire population, there were more than 16 million lives lost. In Poland, there were more than 5 million casualties; more than 15 percent of the country's population perished. During the six years World War II raged on, roughly 80 million people died—4 percent of the world's population. As a rabbi once put it to me, "While the rest of the world was counting their dead at the end of World War II, the Jewish people were counting those alive."

The war led to one of the largest migration movements in European history. Leaders were redrawing borders, and those who were still alive were displaced all around the world, from South Africa to Australia to Kazakhstan, Shanghai, Palestine, and New York. International relief agencies were founded to develop plans to help the millions of stateless people. Talks of repatriation and family reunification were a key part of these conversations—who would be able to return to their native countries, and who would have to find a new home. Families had been murdered, homes occupied, new identities formed, and hundreds of thousands of young people, like Hana, were arriving on doorsteps around the world, hoping to start anew.

A rumor circulated around Sweden that any person who was forced to flee Denmark because of the Nazis could return and gain citizenship. So Hana decided to join the thousands of other Danes eager to go home. As if pressing rewind on a tape player, she found herself once again quarantined in southern Sweden and sleeping on a straw mattress. "There was so much, too much, going on—people were moving from here to there," she told me. "The trains were full. Everyone was a displaced person, particularly the people who survived the concentration camps. And it was very important to become a citizen of something. So I returned to Denmark, and when we got back to Denmark, they interned us again. They processed us again."

Hana was given a temporary visa to stay in Denmark and received a job working in an office that helped those who had been displaced by the Nazis. "I couldn't have asked for anything better," she said of this placement. "I was to take care of Danes who had fled to Sweden like I had or who had been deported to Theresienstadt. No Danish Jews were brought further than there. These Jews came into the office to reclaim their possessions. People had taken care of their apartments and watered their plants. They didn't steal anything or cause any damage. This did not happen anywhere else in the world."

It was the first time in Hana's life that she was making money. Her office job paid her enough that she could rent a room in someone's private home. She was twenty years old, and all she could think about was going back to Czechoslovakia. "But you have to understand," she said to me, "all of these years, I was a citizen of nothing, and it is very difficult to move around without citizenship. I wasn't a Danish citizen. That rumor was false. You didn't become a Danish citizen. I wasn't a Swedish citizen. I wasn't a Czech citizen. I was nothing."

So a mutual friend connected her to Bernd Drucker—a German Jew who had made himself a home in Denmark. He was a lawyer who was helping victims of the Nazis claim reparations after the war. Like Hana, he had escaped to Sweden in 1943. They began dating, and he helped her get a plane ticket home; it would be her first time flying in an airplane.

"There were two plans," my grandmother said. "One was to see who was left, and the other was to show them that I had become something."

CHAPTER 9

SUCH A CREEPY FEELING

Almost all members of the family, both on my father's and mother's side were exterminated in concentration camps, even my great-grandfather, whom I remember vividly. Each time we, as children, visited him, he gave us chocolate candy, but the most vivid impression is that he always blessed us and recited the blessings over our bowed heads. Even as a toddler and later as a child, I was convinced that nothing bad will happen to me for a long time, after his hands have been laid upon my head.

—HANA'S DIARY, 1986

I wish I could see Prague through the eyes of other tourists. But for me, this city serves as a museum and a reminder of a history long gone. Two-thirds of Prague's Jewish community perished in the Holocaust. More than a quarter million Czech Jews were murdered. When I walk into the Jewish buildings, I find my great-grandparents' names on the lists of those deceased. And when I pass through the Old Town Square, I notice the store where my great-grandfather once made his living. It is now a high-end glass shop that foreigners ride by on their Segways. Prague is the place where the black-and-white images I see in my head clash with the Technicolor hues of tourism. There are castles, impressive theaters, and baroque buildings that have become hostels. It is strange to feel as if I am the only one in a dense herd of urban explorers who sees the streets for what was and not what is.

As I had done in Denmark, I stayed in Prague for about five weeks. Every day, I walked from my borrowed apartment to the Old Town Square and back again. I sat in cafés and wrote lengthy journal entries. I requested interviews with individuals from the Jewish community and tried to make friends with other expats. On Friday nights, I visited different synagogues. I photographed museums and wandered along the river, watching the lives of strangers and attaching my own stories to them.

One day, while I was visiting the Jewish quarter to conduct an interview, a burly man with thick facial hair stood at the corner of a busy intersection watching me with intense curiosity. His flat-brimmed hat matched his gray Dickies pants, which were folded at the bottom. They grazed the top of his black Adidas sneakers. His keys dangled from his belt with authority, yet he still managed to blend in with the other tourists and locals. He spoke into the collar of his coat while glancing down at his shoes. He walked up and down the street, slowly and intentionally, before coming directly toward me. His head turned to scan me from the ground up. He was guarding the Jewish community center, and I was leaning on its wall, waiting for a Czech man named David. From what I was told by a mutual friend, David was around my age and also a grandchild of Prague's Jewish history. He had offered to meet me for lunch.

"Who are you meeting?" the security guard asked me.

"David," I replied.

He nodded before asking, "Is he a friend of yours?"

I nodded, leaving out the fact that I had never met him.

Then he asked me for David's full name.

Satisfied with my preinterrogation answers, I was passed off to a man with a hipster-style beard. He wore blue jeans with brown boots and a black beanie on his head. He must have been close to my age as well. His bright-blue eyes struck me. He asked me about my Jewish identity and wanted to know if I had had a bat mitzvah and where it was. I told him that my grandmother was from Prague. He was unimpressed.

Many minutes later, David arrived. He was shorter than I was, with deep-set eyes and a kippah atop his head. We greeted each other, and then he had me follow him inside the main building for the Federation of Jewish Communities in the Czech Republic. My bag was scanned and my body patted down before I walked through a metal detector. "Don't worry," David said. "In here you are safe." I entered a big hallway that was bustling with people; flyers for services and lectures were pinned to the wall. I wasn't sure if being of Czech Jewish descent meant that I automatically belonged. "If I was a general tourist who just wanted to come see this building, would they have let me in?" I asked him.

"I don't think so," he replied.

"Even though I am Jewish?" I retorted.

"Well, if you don't have a legitimate reason to get inside, like an appointment or something . . ."

"Curiosity isn't enough of a reason?"

"No, not at all."

"I feel as though that's unfortunate for general tourism," I expressed, bothered by the fact that not just anyone could visit, considering I could walk into any church in the country.

"I worked in security for three years, and I remember we had some terrorist attempts. It's a very popular potential target," he responded with assurance.

"Why is that?" I asked, knowing the most paranoid and legitimate reason.

"First of all, to do an attack on a Jewish site or a Jewish target," he explained. "And second of all, to harm the economy. This is the most visited place in the country, these streets here—the Old Town Square, the Jewish Quarter, Prague Castle, and Charles Bridge. And if this would leak into the media, it would harm the economic situation and tourism, and the current situation in the Jewish community as well."

He led me into the dining hall, which also served as a meeting room. That evening, Sir Nicholas Winton's daughter was coming to speak. (Winton is known for his role with the Czech Kindertransport; he helped save nearly seven hundred Czech Jewish children by helping them get to England. There is a statue of him at the main train station in Prague.) David and I sat down at a table, and he handed a waiter two small tickets, one for each of us, in exchange for a hot kosher meal. There were plenty of other tables, mostly filled with men looking down seriously at their food. The server silently placed dishes and silverware in front of us and returned a minute later, just as quietly, to ladle soup into our bowls. Pieces of carrots and peas floated on top. It looked just like the "Sabbath Soup" that Sergiusz and I ate after visiting Auschwitz.

David and I spent the afternoon together. He introduced me to prominent members of the Jewish community—rabbis, Holocaust survivors, men in leadership roles. We talked about the fact that our grandparents likely knew each other and swapped experiences of growing up Jewish in our respective countries. At the end of the day, we parted ways and promised to meet again.

When Hana returned to Prague in 1946, she found a few living relatives—a couple of aunts who were spared from the extermination camps because of their interfaith marriages, as well as Eva, her younger cousin, who Hana understood to have been hidden in a convent. There was also her beloved Uncle Pavel, who survived by walking through Czechoslovakia and Poland and into the Soviet Union, where he enlisted in the Soviet Army. None of these survivors embraced or even acknowledged their Judaism after the war. It remained hidden even from the next generation. "These were the people who told me the fate of my parents and of Petr," my grandmother told me. "So I knew that they were gone. But you know, you walk on the streets and you think, maybe you'll meet your brother, but I wouldn't even recognize him. I wouldn't even know how he looked like. Like a little kid. Everybody freezes in your mind. You cannot visualize how they would look older."

The grief consumed her immediately. "Many, many years later, the psychologists put a label on everything," she said. "And the label was 'the guilt of the survivor.' And I had that guilt of the survivor, even though I didn't know that's what it was. I still today, fifty years later, question myself. There must have been a purpose. And then I say, 'Maybe life is just a lottery.'

Maybe it's random.' And I believe that more and more the older I get, because there are righteous people who die, and there are criminals who keep on living. And I felt very guilty, and when I found out what happened to my parents, I did slash my wrists, but not deep enough. I said to myself, 'Why, why am I alive? I don't deserve it.'"

I spent time with some of these distant family members in the Czech Republic. Eva still lived in Prague, and I would visit her weekly. She often made me *knedlíky*, a traditional Czech dish that smelled of my childhood. The dumplings stuffed with plums were a staple in my grandmother's kitchen. Eva didn't talk much about the war; she was more interested in hearing about my travels and love life. I also spent time with Marta—Pavel's daughter, who was born a year after the war ended. There is a lovely photograph in Hana's archive of her holding Marta as a child. Marta now lived in Brno, and her English was about as good as my Czech, which meant we knew about a dozen words in common. For the days she hosted me in her home, we communicated through bright-green Post-it Notes and Google Translate.

I felt like an intruder in Prague. Hitler envisioned this city as a museum to the Jewish people—a place dedicated to what he had destroyed, or in his eyes, what he had built. On some days, I felt like he had succeeded. While there, I was hosted by a young woman who was kind enough to let me live in her spare bedroom. She was one of the few of my generation who was active in the Czech Jewish community. I never felt comfortable in her apartment, but then again, I never felt comfortable in the country. These were the days when no one asked who I was, where I was going, or where I was coming from. This was the place where grief and ghosts took me by the hand.

At night, I would sit on a weak wooden chair and edit whatever pictures I had taken that day. I had a twin bed that was more like a cot squeezed next to a black wooden desk. My pillow was small but functional, its case printed with classic pink roses. I stacked my clean clothes on a piano in the corner of the room and kept the rest of my belongings hidden in my backpack. Dusty books lined the shelves. They were old but held modern ideas for their time. The room's window was partially covered by a shower curtain, and the panels of naked glass showed my bare reflection every time I changed my clothes. I fell asleep to the sounds of the former Czechoslovakia playing a melody outside. The country sowed chaos in my subconscious. My dreams scarred me with their stories.

In one dream, I was back in Boston. My friends were too busy to care that I had come back. They literally looked right through me, as if I were a ghost in my own home. The only one who recognized me was my sweet dog, who nestled her head into my chest and took my finger into her mouth, like a teething child seeking the security of its mother. I often woke up with a jolt, my skin sweaty. I would turn to the right and face the wall, then to the left and stare at my backpack. I would touch one foot with the other and tell myself that I was okay.

The nightmares got progressively worse as my time in Prague went on. I remember one night I woke up certain that the building was on fire. I ripped the blanket off, drew my knees to my chest, and rocked back and forth like the men I had seen in prayer at the synagogue the previous week. I took one breath after another until the sun rose and day broke.

During the days, I learned to fear the city more and more. Prague stopped being new and exciting. I stopped feeling curious about what people were saying in Czech and began to feel more sensitive, nearly angry, when I heard people speaking in English. I didn't want to hear their thoughts. I resented the conversations they had with friends over coffee and cake as I sat alone nearby, staring at my computer, reading and rereading my grandmother's words. "I had such a creepy feeling, and I really, really didn't want to stay," she had said about being back in Prague. "But I had nobody in Denmark. I had nobody in Sweden."

———————

Hana carried a stateless passport after the war. It was called a Nansen passport, and it held her Danish visa, which permitted her to be out of Denmark for only six months if she wanted to return. She got the visa extended once, though, and while in Prague, she enrolled in Charles University and studied linguistics. "I studied Danish and Swedish," she told me. "It was the easiest thing for me to do." She collected the forms and documents that confirmed her parents' and brother's deportation, first to Theresienstadt and then to Sobibor. She gathered the family photo albums and found the letters her parents had saved from the early years of the war. Her teenage handwriting stared back at her. She looked at the postage, sent from Denmark and stamped with the Nazi seal of approval.

"It was difficult because my aunt, who I was living with, really wanted me to stay," my grandmother told me. "She was the only Dubová left, aside for me. She was very much against me leaving, going back to Denmark and to the unknown. I had no job in Denmark. I had nowhere to sleep in Denmark, but I didn't want to stay in Prague. I knew Communism was a big threat, and I said, 'I'm not going to live under an oppressive system.' I said, 'I'd rather take the risk,' and at that point, I had enough confidence that I could make it on my own."

I knew I didn't have to make it on my own. I had Sergiusz. Without intending to, he returned to me a European identity that had been washed away by two generations of assimilation in the United States. Whenever I returned to Poland, he would meet me at the train station, the airport, or the bus depot, no matter the time of day or night. He would welcome me back to our little studio in Warsaw or to his parents' home in Poznań with homemade bread, a hot meal, and craft beer. Over dinner, he asked me questions and listened to my stories for as long as I wanted to share. Somehow, he knew when to talk to me and when to leave me alone, or more so, he knew when I *needed* to be on my own. I like to think I could have done it all on my own though, without his help. I have the confidence, like my grandmother had, that I could have navigated my way around Europe without anyone's advice or insight, without a helping hand or a hand to hold. But there is one place I am certain I never would have seen without him. I would never have gone to the end of the world and back, to the site of my family's murder, to Sobibor.

It didn't take long to get there. It was just shy of a four-hour drive from our apartment in Warsaw. We drove along lonely state roads and through simple villages, passing stretches of desolate, frozen farmland. It was a Poland I hadn't seen. Prostitutes waited at intersections. Rundown shacks sat next to modern houses. Farmers stood on the corners conversing with their neighbors. Older women biked past us and young kids chased their family's chickens. We drove so far east in Poland that we were just a few kilometers from Ukraine, just a few short miles from the border of the European Union.

I didn't want to visit here. To call it hell would be too kind a word—this place of mass murder, of hopeful extinction, of intentional suffocation. If the trees could talk, they would tell you what they saw. They would tell you of the smell of ash and the sounds of gunshots. They would tell you that they saw my great-grandparents being stripped and shot. They would tell you that they witnessed Hana's younger brother dig his own grave. The trees would tell you that he was only thirteen.

As Hana found refuge in Denmark, her family in Czechoslovakia was being conditioned for death. She explained the Holocaust like this, "You are slowly being peeled off like an onion. You are slowly losing first your privacy, your schooling, your income, your possessions. You are being conditioned to worse and worse situations. You are saying, 'This, too, shall pass. We can live with this.' But you are being conditioned to live a subhuman life. And when you are looked at like subhumans, no one has trouble killing you."

Sobibor was designed with intention, shaped like a rectangle, and built in a thinly populated region. The barbed wire fence was woven with branches, and the extermination camp was surrounded by trees. The same trees that let in the winter sunlight as Sergiusz and I approached the site. The Nazis knew that they must enclose death. "They were shot," my grandmother told me. "In Sobibor, they had these trenches that they had to dig. They were undressed, and they were shot. But maybe it is so, that if they were shot forty-eight hours after they arrived, they saved themselves a lot of suffering."

The men and women were separated upon arrival. The children went with the women, so if they were shot, perhaps my great-grandmother had watched her son die. They could have also been gassed. Around five hundred Jews were poisoned at a time. It took twenty or thirty minutes for each round. Other Jews, the ones forced to stay alive, were ordered to take the dead bodies from the gas chambers and pull out any gold teeth before throwing them in a mass grave.

For a Nazi extermination camp, Sobibor only functioned for a short time. But in the seventeen months between May 1942 and October 1943, about 250,000 Jews from Poland, France, Germany, the Netherlands, Czechoslovakia, and the Soviet Union were killed there. Sometimes when prisoners arrived, they would be forced to write letters to relatives to say that they were at labor camps. Once the letters were sent, they were immediately murdered.

Sergiusz and I pulled the car over to the side of the road. We saw a few simple houses and a set of train tracks. There were no cars. There were no faces. There were no sounds. It was quiet. But it was not empty. There was a manicured path featuring a small exhibit that told about the deaths of the prisoners. Small rocks lined the way, each placed in front of a pine tree. I am told that the Nazis called this the "Road to Heaven." Each stone bore a name. Some stones said, For the Unknown. Sergiusz's footsteps haunted me. And my footsteps haunted him. With every step, we broke the perfect layer of undisturbed snow.

We walked a short distance into the woods before being stopped by a simple string tied between wooden benches. The remains of gas chambers, bones, and other objects belonging to the victims had recently been found. I needed to get away from this place. It wasn't like visiting Auschwitz, with the voices of hundreds of international visitors ringing in my ears. Stepping back in Sergiusz's footprints, I decided I didn't need the pictures I had planned to take.

Then a dog's bark echoed across the empty land and broke time. Pictures flashed through my mind—pictures of German Shepherds, Nazis, brutality, and fright; pictures of burnt bodies, starved bodies, murdered bodies; pictures of my forefathers' bodies. The bark reverberated off the rusted railroad tracks and through the bare branches. It was as if the dog were telling us we had no reason to be here.

Sergiusz touched my waist as he unlocked the car. We turned on the engine and shut the doors, straining our necks to look back toward a pale-pink house that had one small window near its triangular roof and a lone door carved into the side. Supposedly it's where the commandant had lived.

The dog was satisfied with our decision. Her stiff tail relaxed as a young girl emerged from the house; her body was protected by a warm winter coat and snow pants as she went to play. In this place, at the end of the world, I was looking at a vision of love that exists only between a girl and her dog. It was a glimpse of familiarity. *I know this love*, I thought. *I have this love.*

Sergiusz and I drove off in silence. We said only, *Let's go home.*

CHAPTER 10

FIVE HOURS, SIX HOURS, SEVEN HOURS

Often I wonder if it all means anything to this generation. If it penetrates, if it leaves any impact . . . What impression do they walk away with? What compassion and understanding do they feel toward an unprecedented event, an incomprehensible black page in history, so long, long time ago? This doesn't concern them at all. They cannot passively relate to this horror. They have their own problems to cope with . . . What does my life, my experience—for that matter, my lost generation—mean to them?

—HANA'S DIARY, 1991

As I neared the end of my year in Europe, I returned, at least once, to every country I had been to. I went on vacation with Sergiusz's family to Italy. I spent a few days in Germany. I returned to Prague, to Sweden, and to Denmark. Of all these places, the country I found to be most alive with my history was Denmark. When I took Sergiusz to visit Sine and her family for a couple days at the end of May 2015, he fell as much in love with their life in the countryside as I did. I remember watching him and Torsten sitting together, watching the sheep graze and the evening sun high in the sky. I was with Sine in the kitchen. Liva was watching TV, Lauge was tinkering with some science project, and Silje was lining up her stuffed animals. It was a quiet moment. Nothing exceptional, but a scene Sergiusz and I would come to reflect on as the vision we hoped for our future.

"I asked Torsten what it was like to live such a quiet existence," Sergiusz told me later that night when we were laying in bed.

"What did he say?" I asked.

"It's good," Sergiusz stated, "He simply said, 'It's good.'"

This became our mantra. "It's good" was our highest compliment for a homecooked meal, a new outfit, a long walk, or whatever brought us pleasure. Our outspoken goal was to build a life we could look out over and simply say, "It's good."

During those few days in Denmark, Sergiusz and I decided that when it came time to have our wedding celebration, which would happen about a year after we married, we would host it on Sine and Torsten's farm. They had a hundred-year-old event house on their property that they often rented out for family celebrations. It would be convenient for his family and symbolic for mine.

Hana only saw Jensine's family once after the war. That was in 1947, when she returned from Prague. Both my grandmother and Rabbi Bent Melchior emphasized that the world was crazy then. "I mean, all of those people who survived the camps—they were stateless and homeless," Bent had said to me. "But nobody wanted them."

Life and death were everywhere. There were upwards of 250,000 Jews living in displaced-persons camps around Europe. The rate of marriages boomed among Holocaust survivors, and between 1946 and 1948, the birth rates in these camps were the highest in the world. It wasn't just the victims creating new life, it was soldiers too. Young men who had survived fighting for their country returned home to their wives and gave birth to the baby boomer generation. (My dad is one of these boomers, born almost exactly nine months after his father returned from fighting for America.) Jensine gave birth as well—to twin girls, Hanne-Lise and Inge-Margrethe (Sine's mom). Hana attended their baptism, and that was the last time they would ever see each other. She left Denmark soon after that and headed back north to Sweden.

A Czech couple named Jiří and Maren Jakerle were the ones who convinced Hana to move to Stockholm in the late 1940s. They had met Hana in 1944, during the final year of the war, and took a liking to her. They invited her to go skiing, took her to concerts, and introduced her to other Czech immigrants in Stockholm, giving her access to a community of fellow refugees who spoke her language. My grandmother said that they were the first people to ever invite her to their home for dinner. "It was really something so wonderful, something unbelievable. I went and bought a big bouquet of roses for them," she recalled. "Jiří and Maren didn't have any children, so they treated me as a daughter. They gave me a feeling that I belonged to a family, that I was a part of a family."

When Jiří and Maren found out Hana had returned to Scandinavia after the war, they secured her a job in Stockholm, finding her a position at a big company called the Aktiebolaget Gasaccumulator, or AGA for short. Hana was grateful for her position, which was operating the mimeographs used to reproduce the engineers' drawings. Every evening, she went home with her hands stained by the blue ink.

There was a nursery on-site for the working mothers, and the food in the cafeteria was free of charge. There were tennis courts and a boathouse with canoes that she could use either before or after work hours. During this time, Hana had friends and lovers. She skied in the winters and hiked in the summers. It had been almost a decade since she had fled Prague, and her life felt fuller than at any other time since the war had begun.

In 1948 two major events provided options for Jewish refugees who, like Hana, were still stateless. The first was the establishment of Israel, but she had already decided that this wasn't right for her. "Let me tell you," she said. "The people who tried to get to Palestine after the war, they first had to go to Cyprus. And I thought, I don't want to be interned anymore. I don't want to be quarantined again. I don't want that."

The second major event was the passing of the Displaced Persons

Act in the United States, a country that had legislated strict immigration laws long before the war even began. Already in 1924, before Hitler had come to power, the US Congress had passed a law limiting total immigration to less than two hundred thousand people a year with the intention of keeping out "undesirable" immigrants, which included Jews, Asians, and Africans. Congress framed the decision as a means of protecting America's "racial stock." These anti-immigrant sentiments only grew more intense during World War II. There was one attempt to get refugees out of Europe, and that was in 1944 with the USNS *Henry Gibbins*, an American troop transport that brought about a thousand refugees to America as special guests of Theodore Roosevelt. Each refugee had to sign a document promising that he or she would return to their home country after the war. It wouldn't be until almost half a decade later in 1948 that the United States passed the Displaced Persons Act, giving permission for an additional four hundred thousand displaced people to immigrate to the United States; about eighty thousand of those visas went to displaced Jews.

So Hana looked toward America, hoping to fulfill her father's desperate wartime wishes. "Jiří asked me if my family had ever applied to go to the United States, and I told him the stories about my grandmother's stepsister in Cincinnati. So he did all the research for me and helped me collect all the necessary paperwork."

Hana got her papers and was given a visa as part of the quota set for Czechs. "But I really didn't care," she stated. "I wasn't in such a hurry, and by the time the visa arrived, I almost didn't want to go. I had established myself in Sweden. I didn't want to start all over again, especially with another language—my sixth. I didn't want to start over not knowing anyone or having a single connection."

Hana was exhausted but thought that maybe in America she could become a stewardess or a translator, so she began learning English. She figured that if life in America didn't work out, she would have six months to return to Sweden.

In 1950, when the war felt both long-gone and hauntingly present, Hana left Sweden. That October, she boarded a boat in Gothenburg that took her first to France and then onward to England. As a tourist, she visited the Eiffel Tower and the Arc de Triomphe. Through the London fog, she peered up at Big Ben and watched the changing of the guard. Then on November 16, 1950, in Southampton, England, Hana stood side by side with other hopeful emigrants and boarded a great ship called the *Queen Elizabeth*. As if it was as simple as turning a page in one of her frayed photo albums, she went from being a fourteen-year-old girl to a twenty-five-year-old woman leaving everything for something.

Her childhood in Prague, the first train ride through Germany, her life on the farm—it was all behind her now, as was her time at the finishing school in Sorø and the traumatic boat ride across the Baltic Sea to Sweden. She waved adieu to her many months living near the Arctic Circle, where she had studied to be a nurse. She temporarily erased the memories of lonely walks through a broken Prague after the war. She tried to stop wondering if her grandparents would have even recognized her had they survived. Her parents' deportation and the fact that her brother was murdered before having the bar mitzvah he dreamed of was pushed aside. Her few remaining family members in Czechoslovakia, her friends in Sweden, her romances, and her childhood courtship with Zionism were all left on the shores of Europe as she boarded a ship to America.

―――――

Before she left for America, Hana had befriended a man named Mosley. She met him while working at the AGA in Stockholm. He was an exchange student from Frankfort, Kentucky, and became her first American friend. "He bought himself a motorcycle and asked me to join him on the back seat," my grandmother said, swooning. "He didn't know one word of Swedish. He was very tall and Black. I was fascinated by his size and his color—and such white teeth when he smiled. I had never known a Black person before."

They made an agreement that while Hana was waiting for her visa, she would teach him Swedish and he would help her learn English. "He told me that Kentucky was right across the Ohio River from Cincinnati, which I knew was where in America I had to go. He told me that he also had some family in Cincinnati and asked if I would bring gifts for them. I agreed and was thrilled that I would know someone in the city."

Hana arrived in New York just after the Thanksgiving holiday in 1950. Her required documents were folded in her bag. Other keepsakes— such as notes from past classmates, letters from lost family members, diaries, and photo albums—were tucked away. She had bought herself a winter coat for the move, as well as a hat and a tailored blue suit; Maren sewed her a shirt to match. Hana wore it with a straight back and her head held high. She still had little grasp of the language and nearly no awareness of American culture. She carried far more trauma than belongings, but willed herself to be optimistic about the future. "The world held so many promises for me. A new country, a new language, new experiences. Although I had not the slightest idea what I will do in America, where I will live, or what I will do for work, it didn't bother me. I always made it," she said.

She spent one night in New York and then traveled to Cincinnati by train. "I had no idea that the country was so big," she recalled. "Every time the train stopped at a station, I jumped up. *Am I in Cincinnati?* I couldn't believe it—five hours, six hours, seven hours, eight hours on the train." She watched as the light bounced off of unfamiliar architecture and folded itself into the skies framed by mountains. She silently etched the landscape into her head with anxious disbelief.

Hana was received at Union Station in Cincinnati by a man named Rudolf Weil. He was a baker, and his wife, Minnie, was the stepsister of Hana's grandmother. They lived in a big house with a big lawn. Like many of their neighbors, they had emigrated from Germany before either of the World Wars and remembered Europe as it was in their little villages at the turn of the century. By this time, Americans were beginning to understand what had happened during the Holocaust. The Nuremberg Trials had taken place, bringing the word *genocide* into the modern lexicon. Nazis had been convicted of war crimes; many were executed, others escaped Europe and found hidden refuges in places like Brazil and Argentina.

Villages throughout Europe were decimated, and entire communities had been murdered. Borders had shifted, democracies had crumbled, and roots had been burned. By 1950, family members in America had stopped wondering if the letters from Europe would ever come again. Collective memories were beginning to form, but as far as I know, Hana and the Weils didn't really talk about it.

When Hana first entered the Weil's home, Minnie brought her to the light switch to show her how it worked. Hana responded with hysterical laughter. She told me she had tears running down her cheeks as she tried to explain to them that they also had electricity in Europe.

Rudolf and Minnie lived with their son, Joe, who was a bachelor in his forties. Hana was under the impression that the parents hoped she would marry him. "What did they think of me? Wanting to marry such an old man," she scoffed. The family's daughter lived down the street with her husband, and the two households shared a party line, which meant that if one household was using the phone, the other could not. Hana thought it was the greatest luxury to be able to call someone, and after a couple of weeks in their home, she asked if she could do just that.

Hana dialed the number of Mosley's family, practicing her English in her head as she waited for someone to pick up on the other end. A man named Ken answered and was delighted to hear from her. She suggested that he come to her house to pick up the gifts.

"Where is it that you live?" he asked.

"Avondale," she replied.

"Oh, no, I cannot do that," he said. Hana gave no thought as to why he wouldn't want to visit her house.

"Why don't we meet in the center square? You'll recognize me," Ken then suggested. "I'll be wearing a green hat."

While Hana was on the phone with Ken, the Weil's daughter listened in and reported back to her parents that Hana had likely dialed a number that was in the Black part of town. "Mrs. Weil kept saying, 'You cannot. You are not permitted to go there,'" my grandmother told me. "I really didn't know much about the prejudices in the United States toward Black people. I said to them, 'I have been all over Europe, and I can go in Cincinnati wherever I want.'" They compromised: she could go, but only if Joe was her chaperone.

Hana and Joe found Ken in the square as promised, wearing his green hat and his Sunday best. She gave him the gifts Mosley had sent. He thanked her profusely and invited her to join him at his parents' home for dinner. When she excitedly accepted the invitation, Joe exploded at her, "You are not going with a nigger anywhere."

Hana said that she would too go, making it clear he could not stop her. She had been on her own for the past eleven years, and no one was now going to start telling her what to do.

Then, right there in the public square, Joe slapped her.

"He hit me," my grandmother said, looking straight into my eyes. "That didn't even happen to me during the war, that someone physically hit me."

Hana left Joe and followed Ken on the bus to his parents' home. She learned that his father was a Pullman porter on the Baltimore and Ohio Railroad and described their house as being immaculate. It was the first time she ever encountered plastic slipcovers on top of slipcovers.

The dinner conversation was warm, although it frequently halted due to Hana's poor English. She did her best to answer questions about what life was like in Sweden, telling them about the short winter days, the long summer nights, and about the many islands that make up the city of Stockholm. At the end of the evening, Hana practiced expressing gratitude in her new language. She then followed Ken to the bus stop and navigated her way home.

She looked out the window as the bus made its way through the Cincinnati night. It was dark now, and she could see her reflection, overlapping with the moving pictures of her new country.

The sounds of her heels clacking on the sidewalk followed her home as she walked from the bus stop to the Weils' house. Each square of cement sent a slightly different tone into the December air. She arrived at the few stairs that led up to the walkway and to the front door. One step and then another guided her to the two suitcases she had brought from Europe. They were packed and waiting for her with an envelope sitting on top. She quietly opened the unofficial piece of mail to find $200 she didn't know her father had sent before the war and a note that read, "We do not harbor nigger lovers."

"So now I ask you," my grandmother said to me, "someone who has never met me in Denmark rescues me during the war. And then someone who is vaguely related to me in Cincinnati, who knows all about the Holocaust and what I went through, kicks me out because I met a Black man on the square? That's what I had come to America for?"

CHAPTER 11

WOMEN HAVE THESE INSTINCTS

[We] held up our heads, our survival by our own wits, our abilities, our ethics.

—HANA'S DIARY, 1991

I followed Hana to Cincinnati in July 2015. I had spent the last ten months traversing Europe, barely covering as much distance as I would in America, but now there was no currency exchange or language barrier. I was in my home country, where history told a different story, where family traumas sculpted by prejudice, discrimination, and genocide were both silenced and memorialized by different groups of people.

I had left Sergiusz in Europe, and both of us were feeling optimistic about how his own immigration process was going. He had diligently collected the required documents and visited the embassies of all the countries in which he had ever resided. Together, we wrote independent statements about our relationship. The government compared our storylines, making sure they matched up before putting a seal of approval on our romance.

Sergiusz was petitioning for a fiancé visa. In the same way that being American made it easy for me to be granted temporary residency in Poland, we expected his application process to go smoothly as long as we fulfilled our promise to marry within ninety days of his arrival. Not unlike what the Weil family did for Hana, my parents agreed to write him an affidavit—a pledge of financial support.

We were both antsy and eager as we counted down the end of our long-distance relationship. We would spend the summer away from each other, wavering between a six and nine-hour time difference, and then on the first of September, we would go home together to my apartment in Boston.

I had returned to an America that was on the cusp of cultural eruption. Headlines broadcast the legalization of gay marriage as well as a racially motivated massacre in a Black church in Charleston, South Carolina. For the previous year, I had watched protests unfold and heard rally cries over the Internet for a more just America, one in which minorities, namely African Americans, could live without fear of being targeted and shot by police. Now, as I began to follow Hana through America, news cycles were repeating the phrase "Nazi ideologies," which felt surreal, and opinion makers were passionately debating the removal of the Confederate flag that was still being raised at the state capital in South Carolina.

While in Cincinnati, I stayed at the Hebrew Union College campus. The dorms were mostly empty in the summer, so I had the fourth floor all to myself. In the mornings, I would chat with the staff. One custodian would often respond to my daily "How are you?" with "The good Lord woke me up this morning, so I can take it from there." At night the sirens wailed through the thick July air, composing an urban lullaby that competed with the Danish TV drama I was watching on Netflix. As I lay on the bottom bunk, clutching my travel pillow, I hoped that Sergiusz would be awake early enough for me to say goodnight.

––––––––––

My grandmother told me that she couldn't remember where she slept the night she was kicked out of the Weils' house. She guessed it was on a park bench.

"Did you think about going back to Sweden?" I asked her.

"No," she replied with certainty. "Number one, I wanted to learn English. And number two, I would have lost face if I came back to Sweden after two or three weeks here just to say that I don't like it. I just couldn't do that."

Instead, she found a place to live on a main street called Reading Road. It was a three-story boarding house with asymmetrical windows. For five dollars a week, she shared a bed with a girl from Kentucky who worked at a dry cleaner's. She searched the want ads and found herself a job as a filing clerk for twenty-five dollars a week.

Hana immersed herself in English as she had done with Danish and Swedish. "I wish I were a wicked witch with velvet violet eyes," she repeated aloud to herself every day, as well as, "Three gray geese went on green grass grazing; gray were the geese, and green was the grazing." She learned how to pronounce the difference between the letters *V* and *W* and got rid of her rolling *R*'s.

"I joined the Jewish community and made a life for myself," she told me. "And I made a friend named Inga who had come from Germany with her mother. Her father was killed in a concentration camp."

One afternoon in 1951, Hana and Inga attended a picnic hosted by the Jewish community where she met a man named Ralph Seckel, a German Jew born in Berlin. He was a year older than Hana and got out of Germany in 1938 with his younger sister. His parents had been wealthy and were able to send the children to live with extended family in New York City, while they survived the war in England. The family eventually reunited in America.

"Ralph began talking to me. My English was *kacha kacha* (so-so)," my grandmother told me. "He said there is an opera on the radio and asked me whether I would like to go to the car with him and listen. I said to him that I was warned in Europe never to go with a guy to his car because they have other things in mind. So he says, 'Okay, so I'll leave the car doors open.' And that impressed me."

Hana and Ralph began dating. He worked as a traveling salesman and drove from his base in Dayton to Cincinnati to see her. During this time, Hana found a new job helping underemployed and underprivileged people receive their social services. "I got a job in a speech and hearing clinic with my accent, where they were supposed to teach proper speaking. So you know, if there is an oxymoron, there it is. I was making thirty-two dollars a week," she told me.

"One day a woman calls up. My English was getting so good that your hair didn't stand up on your head when I spoke. So this woman says to me, 'I am sorry, I have to cancel my husband's appointment because he passed away.' So I said, 'Where did he go to?' I had no idea about that expression—'passed away.' She says, 'What do you mean? I just told you, he passed away.' So I said, 'Is he coming back next week?' And these are things that happen when you are on your own and nobody teaches you the ropes, even if you know the language."

Hana didn't adapt to Cincinnati as she had to Denmark and Sweden. "I hated Cincinnati. I hated it," she said. I hated the heat and the summer and there was no air conditioning. My lipstick totally melted down the dresser. It was so hot and so humid, and coming from Sweden, I was really not used to that."

Most of what I know about my grandmother's social life in Cincinnati comes from one photo album she left behind. It is a beautiful leather-bound album that begins with photographs of her on the ship that took her to America. The only information about the people within these pages comes from my grandmother's captions. Ralph isn't anywhere to be found.

"Inga would always tell me how much she thought that Ralph liked me. But there was something sitting wrong inside of me," my grandmother said about the suspicions she had of Ralph. "Women have these instincts. He called me one day and said that he had to see me tonight. I told him that if this is about another woman, just say goodbye. I don't want to hear about it. He said that it was about another woman and told me that he was engaged to someone in New York City and had been the entire time, but he had to see me tonight. So I broke it off and decided to leave for San Francisco. I said to myself, I make thirty-five dollars a week. I spend five dollars a week for my sleeping room. I eat here for ten cents or twenty cents. I will save enough money to go to California. I want to see the city where I heard there was a big earthquake once upon a time."

———————

I followed the address on my grandmother's immigration documents to the house where she lived with the Weil family and then found the address of the boarding house on a stamped letter. They weren't far apart. Some of the neighbors had manicured lawns lined with flowers; other homes were left vacant, with boarded up windows, concave roofs, and rotting wooden rocking chairs on the front porches.

In the years after Hana left Cincinnati, Avondale, like many American neighborhoods, experienced white flight. In simple terms, the white middle class moved out as African American families moved in. For me, the whole neighborhood felt like a vestige of the past. I walked around quietly with my camera, wondering what it had *actually* felt like for Hana to be kicked out of her family's home. She left behind no diaries from this time in her life; the versions of this story that I know are all layered with fifty years' worth of reflection.

I left the city on a sweaty day in mid-July. I sat at the bus station in Cincinnati, ready to head north to Chicago, where I would board the California Zephyr, the iconic train my grandmother took out west in 1951. I had been looking forward to this leg of the trip since I started traveling nearly a year before. It was my country, now, that I would cross—the country that Hana chose.

My backpack was as heavy as it had been all year, simultaneously building my muscles and breaking my back. The fifty pounds I carried from place to place consisted of typical necessities as well as a yoga mat, a tripod, and a fair amount of camera gear. On my chest, I carried another backpack that held my laptop, books, and the various travel documents—from the past and present—that were relevant for this part of my trip.

People often commented on my appearance, but it happened far more in America than in Europe. "Are you in the military?" a man asked me as I stood in line waiting for the bus that would take me to my transfer in Dayton. "You don't see women that strong who aren't in the military." I gave a fake smile and turned to see a potbellied man finger thick globs of cheese from his pizza into his mouth. A scrawny white woman in front of me, who reeked of stale booze, kept turning to tell me her racist secrets. "Last time I had to sit next to a Black person, but today, I am going to sit next to you. Make sure you stay close to me," she slurred. I pursed my lips and said nothing. Screaming children competed with the sounds of mounted televisions. Usually I hate it when the news blares in public spaces, but today was different. The Confederate flag was coming down from the South Carolina state capitol. The legislative battle that began nearly a month before in the wake of the Charleston shooting had led to change, even if it was just a symbolic one. I noticed that most of the people around me were oblivious to American history in the making as the country began to right its wrongs.

Every war story starts with a love story. And perhaps it is fair to say that it is a love story that starts a war—the love for oneself, for freedom, for choice, for power, for the illusion of security. Often our self-love is overpowered by the yearning to be loved by others. My grandmother's first love story was with Dáša, but her greatest love story was with travel. She found romance in the unknown. She used the same curious tone when talking about her trips to China, Jordan, and Nova Scotia as she did when she told me her story of war. She spoke about train rides as if swooning over a charming man. She bragged about the mountains she climbed and the cold lakes she swam in. "I was quite adventurous," she told me. "And I did it on my own."

One of the most prized possessions I found in her archive is a studio photograph of four generations of women from my family taken in 1929. It traveled with Hana wherever she went. The eldest in the picture is my great-great-great-grandmother whose last name was Reichová. She has a wrinkled face and wears her hair back in a sleek bun. Then, there is my great-great-grandmother Maria Fialová and my great-grandmother Emilie Dubová, both with short wavy hair, styled fashionably for the late twenties. The youngest is Hana as a four-year-old child in a beautiful crepe de chine ruffled dress. The women are posed sitting across from each other, the two eldest gazing at the two youngest. Their faces are round, like my own, and pale in color, also like my own.

"The newspaper in Prague even printed the photograph," my grandmother told me about this portrait. "They wrote a riddle as a caption: 'Two grandmothers, three mothers, two granddaughters, one great-grandmother,

Emilie Fialová married Josef Dub in 1924 when she was nineteen years old (this is their wedding photo). They had Hana in 1925 and a year later moved from Kolín to Prague.

This is Hana and her younger brother, Petr. "I loved, loved, loved him dearly," she once said. "I really was a protective big sister . . . He could have been something."

Hana; her brother, Petr; and her mother and father, Emilie and Josef. This is the last photograph I have of the four of them together. It was taken in 1939, just before Hana left Nazi-occupied Czechoslovakia.

Hana and her *chaverim* in Denmark, the group of friends she left Czechoslovakia with for refuge in Denmark. Hana is standing on the far right and Dáša, her first boyfriend, is in the back row, second from the left.

Hana soon after she arrived in Denmark in 1939.

Me in Denmark in 2017. This photo was taken by Liva Christiansen, the great-granddaughter of Jensine Nygaard.

The Danish countryside in February 2017.

My mom began following in my grandmother's footsteps even before I did. Here are the two of them together in Prague in the early 1980s.

Hana and Ralph's three children: my mom (middle) and her sister and brother, Nina and Peter, during the early 1990s in Peter's home in Pennsylvania.

Hana and Ralph in the 1960s. They were married for twenty-five years before divorcing in the late 1970s.

From Hana and Ralph's three children came seven grandchildren. From the left: Ross, Yoel, Elana, Rachael, Jesse, Daniel, and Emily.

This is one of my favorite photographs of my nuclear family—my mom, Janet; my dad, Dennis; me; and my younger brother, Jesse, in the mid 1990s. The photograph was taken by a newspaper photographer outside our home in Boston.

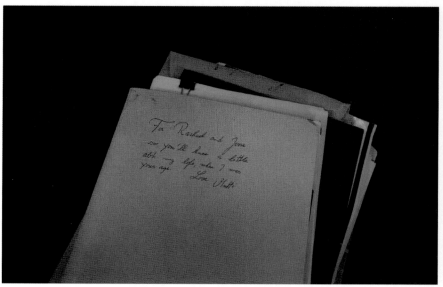

In my grandmother's archive, I found this folder addressed to my brother and me. It reads, "For Rachael and Jesse, so you'll know a little about my life when I was your age. Love, Mutti."

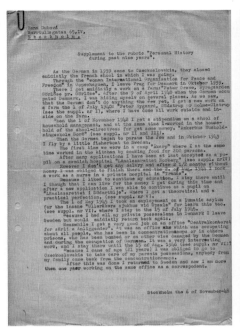

In my grandmother's archive, I found this piece she wrote in 1948 that tells her personal history.
A teacher must have helped her as the writing is at a far higher level than her English was at the
time. On the right is the last picture I have of Hana's parents and younger brother, Petr, before they
were deported in 1942, first to Theresienstadt concentration camp and then Sobibor extermination
camp, where they perished.

Hana in 1941, outside
Jensine Nygaard's home in
Denmark. She had recently
turned sixteen.

My mom embraces Jensine Nygaard in September 2013. Through the wonderful web of journalism, our families connected in 2012. Knud-Arne, Jensine's youngest child, and I stand nearby. Photo by Danish journalist Jan Jensen.

The Danish countryside as seen from Sine Christiansen's farm. August 2016.

Per-Arne and Marianne Persson's daughters show me the exact place along the Swedish shore where my grandmother's refugee boat was spotted after the night lost at sea in 1943. This was the first day I met their family. March 2015.

Outside Per-Arne and Marianne Persson's home in Beddingestrand, Sweden, are over a dozen and a half flags from different countries. This is the house that Hana first walked into after making the illegal crossing from Denmark to Sweden in 1943. August 2016.

This is Per-Arne Persson in 2016. On his sixth birthday, he spotted the refugee boat that my grandmother was on and ran to tell his father, thus saving the lives of the nineteen people on board. Until the day of his death, his home and the artifacts and memories he filled it with told the story of the 1943 rescue.

A 2016 self-portrait on the beach in Beddingestrand, Sweden, where my grandmother first arrived in 1943 during the rescue operation of the Danish Jews.

Sergiusz and I began dating when I started retracing my grandmother's journey across Europe in 2014 but were friends for a long time before. This 2010 photograph, taken by our dear friend Steven Bernstein, is of Sergiusz and me during our final days studying abroad in Jerusalem.

Of the thousands of Jews saved during the 1943 rescue in Denmark, many ran through these woods, which are north of Copenhagen. But after a raid occurred and roughly eighty people were deported to Theresienstadt, refugees like Hana were sent farther south. I took this photo on September 29, 2018, exactly seventy-five years after the Jews were warned to flee.

Sobibor extermination camp. This is where my family—Hana's parents and younger brother—were murdered by the Nazis. February 2015.

Sine, Torsten, Liva, Silje, and I watch the sun set from the farm in Denmark. March 2015.

This is one of my favorite photographs from the We Share the Same Sky project. It is of Liva Christiansen (Sine's daughter) in the back of her family's car during a 2016 family road trip. She is almost thirteen years old in this picture, close to my grandmother's age when she fled home.

I met Rabbi Bent Melchior for the first time in February 2015 when I visited his home and announced that he escaped Denmark with my grandmother in 1943. Over the years, Bent has become one of the most important people in my life (and my adopted grandfather). This photo is of us outside of his Copenhagen apartment in 2019. Photo by my We Share The Same Sky podcast co-producer, Erika Lantz.

Crossing the United States by train (for the second time) in May 2017.

This was Sergiusz's and my unofficial engagement shoot, taken just weeks after he immigrated to the United States. He is wearing his iconic yellow T-shirt with the clown vomiting the rainbow. Photo by our friend Evey Wilson.

Here are Sergiusz's parents with my mom and dad near their home outside Boston. The picture was taken the first time they met, just a few days before Sergiusz and I got married in Maine. From the left: Danuta (my mother-in-law), Dennis (my father), Janet (my mother), and Aleksander (my father-in-law).

On August 27, 2016, nearly a year after Sergiusz and I were legally wed, some of our nearest and dearest from over six countries gathered on Sine's farm for our wedding celebration. Photo by Tracie Van Auken.

This painting is of four generations of woman—Hana and her mother, grandmother, and great-grandmother. It was painted in 2015 by Stephen Gibson, whom I met on an Amtrak train while following my grandmother's story across America. The painting was inspired by one of my grandmother's photographs.

Sergiusz died just a month after our wedding celebration in Denmark. Here I am in our bedroom, sorting through the artifacts of our life together, which felt like it had evaporated in front of me. Photo by our friend Meghan Dhaliwal. October 2016.

My grandmother Hana Dubová in America in the 1950s, looking fierce and beautiful. This isn't how I knew her when I was a child, but how I remember her now.

one great-granddaughter—how many people are there altogether?' The next day the photograph was published as the answer. I don't have the newspaper clipping, but in my album from 'home,' I have this beautiful brown-and-white photograph."

Hana carried this picture with her everywhere—from Denmark to Sweden to America. The photograph crossed more borders than many people do in a lifetime. The four generations of women traveled with her over two thousand miles across the United States—from Chicago to San Francisco, with stopovers in Denver and Salt Lake City. "I took the California Zephyr," my grandmother said of how she got from the Midwest to the West Coast. "It was the most magnificent thing. It was a train with two floors. And it had a glass enclosure so you could see the whole countryside. I had never seen such a big, big countryside."

I don't know as much about Hana's early life in America as I do her life in Europe. There were fewer letters written and even fewer letters saved. I have no diary of hers from that time either. But from this 1951 cross-country trip I have a beautifully penned letter she wrote to a friend in Cincinnati once she got to California:

Dear Lili,

As you see from the stationery, I am staying at the YWCA in San Francisco. Although I have been here only three days, I know that "This is the Place" as Brigham Young said when he arrived at the Salt Lake Valley after a long, tiresome journey.

In spite of your good wishes at my departure, I know that in your heart you thought that I was a little out of my mind to give up my job and room and take a train alone to an unknown place—a young girl without any contacts, any friends or relations. I remember how relieved you and your mother were when I told you that I bought a round-trip ticket just in case. But let me tell you that although that ticket is still in my possession, although I do not have a job—and it is most important that I get one soon—although I do not have a room of my own, I am going to stay, and I am convinced that I am doing the right thing.

But let me tell you about the wonderful trip before I get to the city at the Golden Gate itself. (I do not know much about the city as of yet.) The trip to Denver was quite uneventful. I stopped in Chicago, where I had to change trains, and managed to take one of those sight-seeing buses, which I usually dislike, but it was the only way to see a little of Chicago. That which impressed me most was the Medical Museum, a unique place where, among other exhibits, is shown the development of Homo sapiens from an embryo to a full fetus. The development of science and medicine from the dark ages to our times could here be admired. It was extremely impressive, and as usual, I felt a little envy and admiration for these outstanding people, who contributed so much in science and medicine for the improvement of our health and social standards.

On the train to Denver, I met in the dining car a gentleman who struck up a conversation with me. I was rather glad to be able to talk to someone, but told him a lie. I said that I am going to visit my family on the West Coast as he might have thought it quite odd if I told him the truth. But I told him that I would stop off in Denver to see a little of Colorado. He was heading for the same city, and we had dinner together after I checked in at a little boarding house. So my first evening there was not too lonesome. The next day I went on exploring the city. The weather was beautiful, a real autumn day. The city is extremely clean. In the park which surrounds the City Hall, the trees had already colorful leaves. From bright yellow to red and rusty brown. It almost looked like different materials from which you create expensive draperies in your workshop. In the afternoon I visited the museum, the library, and took a streetcar to the outskirts of the city. Just got on one and rode to the end stop and then back again to the opposite side of the city. Again I got the same impression of a clean, well-organized city with friendly people and hardly any slums. I saw the Jacob Riis TB hospital over which entrance are inscribed these words: those who enter may not pay, those who pay may not enter. The building from the outside looks like a luxurious hotel. When you enter, there is not the typical hospital smell which usually strikes your nostrils. The walls of the corridors are decorated with modern paintings, and this gives you immediately an impression of a place of peace and well-being. I imagine that even the critically sick would have a feeling of confidence and hope for recovery upon entering this building.

The next day I took a limousine trip to Pikes Peak. We were five tourists and a driver. One was an elderly couple, the man constantly smoking a big fat cigar which he hardly took out of his mouth; it seemed to be glued to his lips; his wife a stout woman wrapped in some expensive fur but extremely jolly and with an unsatisfied curiosity, such as asking the driver at each junction about the direction of route B or X without waiting for an answer before popping another question. The two others were a young French boy and a girl who came to this country on student exchange. I was extremely pleased to have these two in our car. It gave me a chance to speak French. Their experiences reminded me a lot of my initial mishaps here in the States. When the trip was over, we were very good friends. They were saving their allowance by "not eating" so that they could explore the country a little on their own. Their diet consisted mainly of fruit and Italian bread. They ate two pounds of apples or peaches or grapes and a loaf of bread each a day at the cost of 40 cents. The rest they spent on excursion trips such as this one.

The first stop was Colorado Springs. It was almost summer down there in the valley, and even the fat lady had to take off her furs. The sun was beating on the car, and we all felt uncomfortable. There was not much to be seen in the town. Soon the car started slowly to climb uphill, and up it went the rest of the trip. The nature started to change. Trees were scarce, the dark brown of the soil was changing to a reddish brown, and soon there were earth formations in a rich red color in fantastic shapes and figures. We reached the Garden of Gods. And it truly is! There are mammoth rocks to which men gave different names according to his imagination, such as three mammoth rocks called Three Graces. To me they looked like "Three Giants," or "Three Monsters." Two others are called Siamese Twins just because they are joined at the bottom. It looks quite grotesque. Still another is called Old Scotchman. It has a human face all right, with tight lips and narrow chin, but it reminds me more of a prudish woman. I took a picture of a Balanced and Steamboat Rock, which is true to its title. I had the film developed, and all [the] pictures came out very well. I will send you some. I only regret that I did not have color film. How different, how much more satisfying to the eye and imagination this nature is than the vast monotonous cornfields of Ohio! It was too late in the season for the annual Indian pageant, which certainly would have been interesting to watch. Even so, I could imagine how the Indians were hiding behind these magnificent rocks, hunted by the white man, or even fighting among their own tribes, jumping on their wild horses and performing their ceremonies in this glorious valley.

We were quite disappointed when we finally reached our destination. Up on Pikes Peak it started to hail, and even some snowflakes came down. The fat lady wrapped herself in her furs, and the rest of us pulled up our collars. We could not see too much. Big pieces of ice were coming down, so back to the car we went and now started a dangerous descent. The climb to the peak had been very curvy, but I had not paid much attention to it as I was full of impressions from the Garden of Gods and leaned back in the seat recollecting again and again the marvels of nature. It was the first time I saw a cactus in bloom (not in a flowerpot but out in the free, and several feet high at that!). There were so many new fantastic things to take in that my mind was far away from the climbing car. But down! Oh!!! Our fat lady almost got an epilepsy attack. Her husband's cigar fell out of his mouth, and the three of us in the back got rather pale. In one of the curves the car suddenly skidded on the road, which by now was extremely icy, and the driver lost complete control of the wheel. Around, around we went in a circle, on a road which almost hung off the cliff. On top of it all, another car came behind us. Nobody was sure whether the other car would be able to stop on the icy road or run into us, which was the only other alternative. But the other driver stopped, and ours regained control. Back went the cigar of our friend, but it was dead, and the *fat lady was unable to speak for the rest of the way, which made the return rather pleasant.*

Three days later, I saw quite a different picture of Mother Nature. First now on this trip I realized how huge, tremendous and full of opportunities this country was and still is. In Salt Lake City, I admitted the courage, the everlasting curiosity, the drive to go on, the exploratory spirit of Man. In the beginning of the letter I quoted Brigham Young. Spending two days in Salt Lake City, I was so impressed by this man who lived one hundred years ago. He was an explorer, a philosopher, a writer, an engineer, and a marvelous architect—and to top it all, a Mormon with 14 wives (and who knows how many children). The entire city is his work. One of the guides while showing the sights of the city cracked a joke stating that when Brigham Young saw the valley and imagined all the possibilities this beautiful place had to offer, he sent a messenger (for the women) with these words: "Bring plenty of women and bring them young." But his actual words while seeing the place from the top of his oxcart on July 24, 1847, were: "This is the place, drive on." (He must have had a stenographer on his staff to recollect his words so precisely.)

The city has broad, straight streets, lined with green trees and white or light-gray houses. The guide's interpretation of the wide streets was that Brigham Young had 14 wives and as many mothers-in-law and built the houses so far apart so that the wives and mothers-in-law could not get in each other's hair. The streets are named First East, First West, First North, First South, First South East, First North West, First West South. Then comes the second in the same order. The first street is the nearest one to the capitol and the 30th, or whichever it might be, is the furthest. The local people claim it is easy to find your way about, but imagine if I, with my sense of direction, had a date at the northeast corner of 5th Southwest Street, the poor fellow would stand there till eternity.

This beautiful city was just a green valley one hundred years ago. Nothing was here except green, fertile land. When Brigham Young and his pioneers arrived in 1847 by oxcart, he saw the possibilities of cultivating such a place, building houses, a cathedral, the Mor-mon Temple (to which I could not get admittance). Impressive not in its majesty but in its simplicity, the Tabernacle is a circular wooden structure. A tremendous organ with huge pipes dominates the center, what one may call the altar. A pin can be dropped there, and the acoustics are so excellent that the sound of it can be heard in the very last row. I attended two organ recitals there, and afterwards walked in the beautiful garden with its green lawns, small ponds with water lilies, and around the famous Seagull Monument. While I was listen-ing to the music and later walking in the garden, I felt like meditat-ing and was convinced that I had done the right thing in going west. I went to the state capitol building, a small replica of the Capitol in Washington, DC, and went to see the Mormon Battalion Monument, where I learned that Salt Lake City was first called Deseret, which means honeybee, the emblem of industry according to the Book of Mormon. Incidentally, the Mormons do not smoke, drink, use coffee or tea. There is not a single bar in the entire city (although there are liquor stores), and on the premises of the Tabernacle or the Temple, one is not supposed to light a cigarette, cigar or pipe.

I went to see the Silver Mine. It is a tremendous place dug in a horseshoe shape with platforms overlapping each other. I saved a piece of stone containing a little silver as they were just blasting a section while I was there. The mine is on the outskirts of the city, and the bus took us back passing the Great Salt Lake. If I had had a swimming suit with me, I would have gone for a swim there, just float, so salty and heavy is the water. This way I only took off my shoes and dipped my feet in it. On the way to the city we saw all the salt beds, miles and miles of white salt on the ground and occasionally piled up in white pyramids. A tiny toy train loaded with salt ran back and forth on small rails to a refinery. No wonder salt is so cheap.

In the evening, I went to a high-class hotel—I forgot the name of it. I took the elevator to the top floor (26th) as I wanted to see the sunset over this magnificent valley. To my relief—as I wouldn't have been able to meet the prices—I was not admitted without escort. But I hid on the terrace, taking in the view of the purple sun illuminating the valley and finally disappearing behind the majestic mountains; the same mountains which man conquered in search for better living and happiness.

Then I boarded the famous California Zephyr to reach my goal. It is a wonderful train with three two-story cars, so-called view cars. The roof of these cars is of glass, and in passing different canyons with terrible names such as Devil's Slide, Suicide Hop, etc., the stewardess tells you, through a loudspeaker, how to take your pictures: at what exposure and opening. I took a whole roll through the car window. These are not developed yet.

In the train, I met a young girl of about my age, and we stayed [together] all the way to San Francisco. She, too, was traveling alone and returning after five years absence to the city she loved. It seems she had an unhappy, short-lasting marriage and was just through with her divorce procedures. I liked her at the first sight and suggested that we take a room together at the YWCA when we arrive in San Francisco, which she agreed to do. Since she knows San Francisco, she will be able to show me around and, as a matter of fact, already has. From the practical point, she can tell me where to look for a room and which sections of the city are undesirable, as I would not know the difference. Actually, I have not seen too much of the city at the Golden Gate. Since our arrival, the weather has been most unfavorable. Rain, rain, rain. Every day, all day long. This prevents me from looking for a room without getting soaked. We both go through the daily papers every day, change our dollars for dimes and spend them either on the telephone or on the streetcar. My plan is first a room, then a job, then an apartment all to myself. I hope my plans will materialize. As a matter of fact, I know they will. You see, the sight of the city while approaching it on a ferry was promising of much good and happiness.

The train goes only to Oakland. Then one has to take the ferry to San Francisco, which puffs its way across the bay under the Bay Bridge, not the Golden Gate Bridge, as I [had] thought. As I mentioned before, I haven't seen too much of the city yet. As I know I am going to stay, I [will] have plenty of time for sightseeing after I get *settled. San Francisco is very hilly, and I love to ride on the cable cars. It is an unusual streetcar with cables underneath and it almost sings pushing its way up the hill, and the breaks scream downhill. One cannot be satisfied with two or three rides but has to repeat them over and over again, and each time there is something new to see. Fortunately, the YWCA is located near a cable car stop so that I can take this jolly means of transportation every day. From the cable car you can see the Golden Gate Bridge, the Golden Gate Park, the Pacific Ocean and the bay, the Fisherman's Wharf. You climb the hills with their luxurious hotels and go through picturesque China Town. The cable car takes you also to Market Street, the downtown area, with its customary department stores, offices and employment agencies. As soon as I learn more about this cosmopolitan, picturesque, friendly, hilly city, I'll write again. In the meantime, be well and give my regards to all our friends and especially to your mother and fiancé.*

Yours,

Hana

P.S. Tell my landlady that in a week I will have a place to live, so she can send me my two suitcases.

I followed Hana the whole way from Cincinnati to San Francisco. I watched the farmland pass me in Illinois. In Iowa, the sky turned from a creamy blue to a disconcerting gray. Crossing the Mississippi River, I felt nauseated as the wind began to whip. My phone lit up with a tornado warning a few miles later. It was completely flat all the way to Denver.

Entering the Rocky Mountains, we passed through dozens of tunnels—one was six miles long. We emerged to rock ridges on one side and a vast mountain range on the other. Over a loudspeaker, the conductor told us that we were near the Continental Divide. I focused my attention on the mountains, hoping I would see a moose or a bear.

I felt like the main character in my own movie. My anxiety sometimes manifested while I watched the world in all its majesty pass me by. I wondered what I would do when I stopped following my grandmother's story and went home to Boston. I was scared of how it would feel to return to routine. Sergiusz texted me often with pictures of the suit his mother was having made for him for our wedding. I texted him pictures of the landscape. When night came, it was like pressing the off button on a television. There was nothing left to watch except the slight outlines of the shapes of mountains and those sleeping around me.

I took deep breaths of fresh, muggy air in Grand Junction, Colorado. And in Salt Lake City, at two in the morning, I watched lovers say goodbye to each other on the train platform. I stretched my legs in Reno, Nevada, and as we rode through the Sierra Nevada, I stared at the giant sequoias, feeling them release their fresh oxygen even from inside the train.

I made friends with a guy named Eric who bought me a whiskey, and Max who lived in Telluride, Colorado, and told me his vision of a world that had "generosity wars," in which people would try to outdo each other with acts of kindness. There was a woman in a bright-red dress who traveled with her pet chameleon named Ruby. And there was Ross, a Mennonite who lived in Oakland, California; he and I played cards late into the night. I overheard things like, "We are somewhere in Iowa, that's all I know," and, "I remember when I used to get out of bed without creaking and moaning," and, "Can I buy a cigarette from you?" The train was full of vignettes of strangers.

There were Amish people with bowl cuts and long beards, and Mormons who were clean-shaven. Some of the travelers around me stayed asleep for most of the day, their half-horizontal bodies covered with the sleeves of their sweatshirts. Other seats were empty but claimed by belongings. There was a young couple with nine children, and there was a twenty-two-year-old Peruvian student. When I told him I was following my grandmother's story, he told me that I was living the American dream.

Across the thousands of miles of land now called America—a land built upon broken dreams and resilience; upon wars and stolen property, strict borders, oppression, racism, and loneliness; upon struggle and exploration; upon the backs of those who risked everything to go in search of something and those who, searching for everything, gained nothing—we were all just people, traveling beside one another.

As we neared our final stop, those of us who were still on the train were eager to arrive. We stood in the aisles stretching our legs and massaging our stiff backs. "I've spent more than fifty-five hours on the train," I told a guy named Stephen Gibson. He and his partner, Carlos, had gotten on the train near Denver, where they had been seeing family. Stephen had a big white beard, and I guessed he was about my father's age, somewhere in his late sixties. Shortly into our conversation, we discovered that we were both artists working with family history. This made us quick friends. Stephen was a painter and re-created black-and-white photographs of his family and friends who had passed away. "Come see my studio," he said. "It's in Oakland, at our home."

I accepted his invitation and did visit. We spent hours talking about how art helps us feel closer to the dead. In looking at his paintings, I learned that he lost his younger brother to polio and his longtime partner to AIDS. He told me about his tremors, which sometimes made it hard to paint, and that he, too, carried HIV. A number of the paintings in his collection were of the friends he had lost to the epidemic. He told me his art was therapy. It was the way he kept people alive.

Sitting in Stephen's home that day with him, Carlos, and their two dogs, Dingo and Django, I felt myself soften a bit. The hard shell of history melted away as we comfortably sat in the presence of the dead. They taught me the power of talking gently about loss.

A couple of months later, after I returned to Boston and Sergiusz moved to the States, a package came for me in the mail. It was covered in stickers that read Fragile. I opened it carefully to find a painting of the four generations of women who had come before me. A typed note from Stephen was printed on a plain piece of white paper. It was dated October 10, 2015, five years to the day after my grandmother's funeral:

Dear Rachael,

I was captivated by the photograph of four generations of women of your family, the youngest Hana. I wanted to know these very strong women more profoundly, and so the inclination to do a painting of them consumed me. The time that

I spent caressing their faces with my brushes and giving them
boundaries with my colored pencils was a moving experience
for me. I hope that this picture conveys the tenderness and
respect I have for these women. My life is enriched through
my experience with them. Thank you for opening the dialog and
inviting me to participate in the vitality of your narrative
creation. It is a joy for me to recognize how much you are a
continuation and validation of these Czech women. Thank you
for the introduction.

Much love,

Stephen

The painting came matted and framed; Sergiusz and I hung it in our
bedroom right away. It is the most precious gift I have ever received.

CHAPTER 12

I TRY TO BE FAIR

Often I dream or think about being with him, having someone to take care of me . . . It's an impossible fantasy I have.

—HANA'S DIARY, 1985

By 1952 Hana had made a home for herself in San Francisco. For thirty dollars a month, she rented an unfurnished apartment that she filled with furniture from the Salvation Army. Every day, she would walk down the hill to work and back up the hill on the way home, watching the fog roll in from the bay. For thirty-five dollars a week, she worked in a morgue, washing the stainless steel tables used for autopsies. She joined a Swedish American club and a ski club. She was also in love with a man named Paul Levine, a Dane with a tall frame, who worked for the Scandinavian Airlines' ground crew. "One day the phone rings," she told me. "It was Ralph—from Cincinnati. He asked if he could come see me, but I told him that I didn't want to be the fifth wheel on the wagon. He told me the engagement didn't work out. I told him, 'Tough for you.'"

Ralph followed her out west anyway, and she hesitantly let him back into her life. "So I said to Paul that I have a 'cousin' who is coming from New York for a couple of days and asked if he would drive him around San Francisco," my grandmother admitted to me. "And of course, the 'cousin' stayed with me."

During those days together, Ralph proposed. "I mean I can lie and can be deceiving, but I try to be fair," my grandmother said as if it was some morally ambiguous justification. "So I told Paul that Ralph was not my cousin and laid out the whole story about how Ralph wanted to marry me. And Paul says to Ralph, 'You know, it's not fair for you to see Hana from New York and me to see her here.' So Paul said that he would not see me for a few weeks so I could clear my head and figure out what I want. I really don't have a short temper, but I got mad. I thought that if a man really wanted me, then he should fight for me. I saw it as him not caring about me."

"Were you in love with Ralph the way you were in love with Paul?" I asked her.

"No, but what appealed to me in Ralph was that he had a family. Paul didn't really have that. I didn't marry him; I married the family."

Ralph's job was in New York, as was his father and his sister. Hana agreed to marry him there under the condition that they would return to San Francisco after the wedding. He agreed, and on October 22, 1952, in a rabbi's study in Queens, Hana got married. She was twenty-seven years old and wore a white suit she bought for herself. "I paid my rent until January first. It was September. I have never seen that place since. I would have loved to stay there, but it wasn't in my cards."

My grandmother gave me a quick synopsis of her life in New York. All three children—Nina, Janet (my mom), and Peter (named for her brother, Petr)—were born in Flushing, Queens, a neighborhood which at that time was predominantly made up of Jewish immigrants. She was naturalized as an American in 1956, the same year my mom was born. "After the war, I wanted twelve children to make up for the amount of people killed," she said with a tone of finality. "I had three and gave up."

And that was that. Our storytelling sessions had come to an end. A few weeks later, she passed away.

I followed Hana to New York City in 2015. The addresses on letters sent to her from abroad led me to Flushing. I hopped on the 7 train at Grand

Central Station and rode it all the way to the end of the line, where I stepped onto a platform lined with multiple advertisements for a casino, alternating languages from English to what I think was Chinese. I walked up the stairs, my face to someone's backside, and held my bag close as I followed the herd of humans from underground into the daylight.

The storefronts were all in languages I couldn't read. And the conversations around me were also foreign; there was rarely a familiar word. Vendors on the street sold live crabs from large white buckets. I peered into one and watched their little claws frantically moving. They looked shocked, as if suffocating from the muggy city air. The flow of people moved just as frantically. Many people wore face masks to protect themselves from pollution as they passed by fish markets, bubble tea storefronts, and restaurants advertising whole ducks for dinner.

I walked down Main Street for half a mile. On my left I passed a 1930s-era post office; it looked like a relic from another time. At the intersection of Lok Lok Restaurant and New Happy Home Furniture, I took a right. A block later, I stared up at Hana's New York abode—a brick row home on Avery Avenue. It had a white awning with a red stripe and looked as if it hadn't been painted since Hana had lived there. Bars on the windows protected the first floor. The fence, which was slightly broken but certainly functional, bordered a rectangle of half-healthy grass and a parking spot occupied by a blue minivan. Planes flew low overhead, coming and going from LaGuardia Airport.

I photographed the house as if I were looking at some Bohemian castle. It was as anticlimactic as I worried it might be. After a year of traveling and crisscrossing international borders and state lines a few dozen times, I was done. I was four hours from Boston. I was basically home. I lingered for a few minutes and tried to make conversation with a man I saw walk out of the house. He didn't care to talk to me, but took my business card as a formality. I looked across the street at a daycare center that had advertisements in what again I thought was Chinese. A quick thought flashed through my head that maybe I could volunteer there, as I had in Denmark at Liva and Lauge's school. I pushed the idea away and turned back to the house where my mom once lived. In the generations since my grandmother had become an American, Flushing, Queens, had transitioned from a community of Jewish immigrants to one of Asian immigrants. In my adopted European homes, life seemed to be a continuation of what had happened long before, but here in America, the stories of past generations were uprooted in order to make space for the next one. So I snapped a selfie and walked back to the subway.

Hana stayed in touch with a few of the *chaverim* after the war. Most of her childhood friends were the only survivors in their families as well. Some of them moved to Israel. Others stayed in Sweden or went back to Denmark. Very few returned to Czechoslovakia to stay. Some went to England, Canada, or as Hana had, to the United States. She remained close with Jiří and Maren though, the couple she had met in Stockholm. After Jiří died, Hana sent an affidavit to Maren to join them in Queens. That was in the late 1950s. After Maren got into an argument with Ralph, she moved to Seattle and married her late-husband's cousin. Hana only saw her once again in her life: in 1967 when they met in Banff, Canada while on vacation. "The Jakerles sure were very important people in my life. I loved them dearly," my grandmother reflected in her 1985 diary.

In the 1980s, when most of the *chaverim* were already grandparents, they had a reunion in Czechoslovakia. That is one of the times my mom accompanied my grandmother back to Europe. She began following in Hana's footprints even before I did. "I felt exhilarated in Europe," Hana wrote after that trip. "I felt a true love seeping into each and every pore of my being. I felt loved and I loved all these wonderful people, who eons ago were important in my life, who knew me as a child, who knew my parents, my brother, my family. It was a different world. Since then I have been so much alone, but here I truly felt I fit in. I felt at home."

Hana's longest friendship throughout her life was Dáša, the boy she was in love with when she fled Prague. After the war he went to Israel for some time before returning to Denmark, where he married and raised a family. He and Hana always exchanged letters and would visit each other throughout the years. There even is a family rumor that my grandmother tried to woo Dáša away from his wife after she divorced Ralph in the 1970s. The two remained good friends until the day he died.

My mom and her siblings became friends with Dáša's children, and now I am friends with the grandchildren, so the relationship lives on. Dáša's son, Michael, often hosted me when I was in Copenhagen. (I was staying with them on the night of the shooting in Copenhagen.) He would generously give me keys to his apartment, and he and his wife welcomed me to come and go as I pleased. We would have family dinners together, and when Ruben, Michael's son, had his first baby, I joked with him that now I felt a pressure to have children with Sergiusz so our families could be friends for five generations.

The intergenerational trauma ran deep with the second generation, the survivor's children, but it eased with the third generation—grandchildren like me, Ruben, and his sister Miriam. "My father thought that he was like the bridge between the past and the future because he was also the only survivor in his family," Dáša's daughter, Eva, once told me. "He knew that if he didn't do the work to write his memoir, the future wouldn't know about his family. But he wasn't the type of guy who could express his feelings. He would hold back. We are four children of his, and I think, in different ways, we have been processing his pain. Unconsciously we have been processing his grief."

My mom has echoed the sentiments of carrying the grief of her mother's generation. It's an inheritance I personally don't often feel the weight of. The way I see it is that time has turned the pain into responsibility. Over the years, especially as I have become more and more entrenched in studying Holocaust history, my mom and I have had to confront this generational difference. Sometimes it makes me feel guilty that I see my own history at such a distance, but as I've told my mom many times, it's the only way I can be so intimate with it.

"How are we going to make a better world if you carry these feelings with you all the time?" she has said to me. "If you feel all those feelings, we can't move forward as human beings. There's joy in the sadness, but there's sometimes prejudice that comes from having certain pain, and everyone has their own. The knowledge is good, but I don't want you to feel what I feel."

Dáša was family to my grandmother. He was not only the bridge to his past for his future generations but a bridge for my grandmother to *her* past. They shared the same native language and knew what each other's childhood homes looked like. They could remember back to summer camp together, to their first kiss and riding bikes by castles in Denmark. They knew each other's families—the ones that they were born into and those that stood in for parents during the war—and they knew each other as parents themselves after the war. Dáša was a constant. His was the friendship that survived, and as long as he was alive, so was a part of Hana's childhood. When he died in 2001, a part of her died too.

I have a number of my grandmother's diaries from later in her life. How she lived in the six and a half decades after the war is as interesting to me as the war stories themselves. There is a diary from 1985 and a couple from the early 1990s. For a long time my mom didn't want me to read these. She was worried that they would change the way I would see my grandmother and our family. "I'll read them like a journalist, not a grandchild," I promised her over and over, knowing what she was protecting. I knew that the words I wanted to read didn't belong to me. Hana wrote them by herself and for herself. Yet here I was, begging to examine every thought my grandmother had left behind as if it would bring urgent answers to a question I didn't even know how to ask.

I know that my mom did in fact rip pages out—especially the ones where Hana spoke ill of Ralph. (They divorced in the 1970s.) "You don't need to read that," she told me. But she did let me read my grandmother's complicated feelings about my mom's relationship with my father. It wasn't just moving away that had made my mom the black sheep of the family; it was also that she was the only one who married outside of their faith. My father's conversion didn't matter to Hana, even though it was something he had wanted to do long before meeting my mother. The challenge had more to do with tradition and culture than religion. Hana feared for her daughter the way that I knew Sergiusz's parents and my parents feared for us. Coming from different backgrounds can make relationships difficult, and parents don't want their children's lives to be difficult. I found my grandmother's concern to be poetic. "Their compassion is endless and their pockets are empty," she once wrote.

My grandmother remarried in 1986 to a man named Bernd Drucker—the man who helped her get the plane ticket from Denmark to Czechoslovakia after the war; she was twenty when they first met. He was the maternal grandfather I knew. (Ralph passed away when I was too young to remember.) On paper, Hana and Bernd's love story was one for the ages. He wanted to be with her and live together in Denmark. She had an appetite for adventure and wanted something more. She told him this, that she didn't plan to stay in Denmark and would likely go to America. He told her he wasn't leaving and that a woman should stay where the man is. She said to hell with that. Finally, he told her that if she didn't marry him, he would never marry. And true to his word, when they reunited in the 1980s, he was still single.

Bernd moved to America soon after they wed. We knew him as a kind man who would gently reply, "It is not necessary," whenever someone asked if he needed anything. In her diaries, Hana expressed her frustration with him, and said that he bored her like he had when they first met. Her biggest grievance was that he got to benefit from the life she had worked so hard to create for herself. In June 1990 she wrote, "[I married him because] I felt that Bernd is well established; that I'll have no financial worries; that we have a common history, knowing each other from the time we were young; that he promised himself when I left for the US in 1950; that he'll never marry anyone else but me. I thought it was both admirable, flattering, but at the same time stupid. I didn't want to marry him then, when I was 25 years old. There was something in his personality which never appealed to me . . . His following . . . his constant indecision, his laid-backness, never taking an initiative, his slow speech, his drifting from the subject in discussions. At that time I wanted someone to take me by the hand and arm and lead me. I always had to fight alone for everything. I had to accomplish [everything alone]. I never had anyone to help me."

Over the years, Hana worked an array of jobs to keep a decent life for her and her children. She taught English as a second language to newly arrived immigrants, she worked as a custodian and as a nurse, and when finances were really tight and her kids were out of the house, she rented out their vacant bedrooms to boarders. In 1985, a year before she married Bernd, she wrote, "I thought that at my age, 60, life would be easier for me . . . I never got anything in my whole life given to me. All I have, I worked hard for. I never got a cent of money, or inheritance from anyone. No one ever took care or interest in me."

———————

I didn't let Hana's struggle with love scare me. When Sergiusz and I decided to get married at my family's place in Maine, right at the edge of Knights Pond, I thought about my grandmother's love of symbolism. Like me, she had also married a European immigrant in the month of October. I found comfort in this coincidence. Had my grandmother been alive, I knew she would have loved Sergiusz. The two of them could tell each other secrets in languages the rest of us didn't know.

Sergiusz and I were married on October 15, 2015, six weeks after he immigrated to America. My father officiated the ceremony, and my brother held the rings. Sergiusz's parents read passages in Polish, which my mother then read in English. We had no guests. We let the autumn leaves be our chuppah and Knights Pond be the pews.

I wore a simple white strapless dress that hugged my figure, and Sergiusz wore brown dress pants, a green tweed jacket, a light blue shirt, tan vest, and gray bowtie. A pocket square brought out the bright red threads woven into the tweed of his jacket. I had never seen him look so confident in who or where he was.

We stayed in Maine for about a week after that. In the same house where I had spent long days playing Monopoly with my brother and chasing newts with my grandmother, I started a new chapter of adulthood. I peered down from the top of the stairs at my newly extended family, sliding my feet back and forth on the wood floor, and thought about the first time I watched my grandmother being chased out of her mind by her memories. I knew so little then, and even with all my years of research, I still wasn't so sure I knew that much. In one of her diary entries from 1990, Hana had written, "As I said to Janet while we were walking to beautiful Knights Pond: We all have a huge love (Janet called it a crater) in our lives, a gaping black void, which will never be fulfilled. Everything has its price. Do we want to live single lives and be alone or married lives with all their pains and disappointments?" From the time she was a teenager to being an older woman, my grandmother wondered if love was worth giving up her independence for. I would be lying if I didn't admit that I worried about this too.

A few weeks before the wedding, Sine wrote and told me that she, Torsten, and the kids were coming to New England for a family vacation. I persuaded her to visit us in Maine. "It will be so perfect," I told her. "You can meet Sergiusz's family and my parents. We can host you, and then next year for the wedding celebration, you will host us."

On a Friday evening, October 16, the five of them pulled up the long dirt road in Maine and joined us. It was just a few hours after we had cut the cake. None of the visiting Europeans, including Sergiusz, had ever experienced New England in the fall. So we Bostonians collected piles of red and yellow leaves for the kids to jump in and made a campfire and introduced everyone to s'mores. We hiked to the top of one of the mountains to show off the view of the ocean and took our guests to a local pub, where they ordered fish-and-chips and with wide eyes counted the two dozen televisions mounted on the walls. During those days together, the Polish Catholics, the Danish Lutherans, and we American Jews all spent time together as if we had always been family. It was serendipitous, it was symbolic, and it was good.

CHAPTER 13

CRISIS BEGINS WITH A BLUE SKY

There is a Czech saying: "A healthy man has many wishes. A sick man has only one."

—HANA DUBOVÁ, 2010

Sergiusz always had an affinity and admiration for America. Before we met in Israel, when he was on the work-study program that had him waitering in a greasy diner in New Jersey, he road-tripped around the country with friends, and at a Walmart in Texas, he bought himself an American flag. He carried those first oil-soaked impressions with him home, packed away next to the thick red-white-and-blue piece of cotton emblazoned with stars and stripes.

That flag hung in his dorm room in Jerusalem and also in his bedroom at his parents' house in Poznań. One of the first selfies he sent me when we started dating was of him standing in his green bathrobe in front of the flag, with his hand upon his heart as if saying the Pledge of Allegiance. I found it strange that he was so enamored with America, but embraced it when he decided to immigrate to be with me.

We settled into married life in Boston with relative ease. He did most of the cooking and I happily cleaned up after him. We started our meals with, "*Smacznego*," a Polish phrase that means "bon appétit," and ended our meals with, "*Tak for mad*," a Danish phrase that means "thanks for food." We put up art and opted not to have a television, making our record player the center of our living room. We had an indoor porch with blankets and pillows on the floor and a rocking chair. We would sit there together almost nightly, smoking joints and watching Anthony Bourdain on one of our laptops. Whenever I needed to brainstorm ideas for the many grants I applied for and never received, Sergiusz would listen. His academic mind would take my tangential words and turn them into succinct statements, making me sound smarter than I felt. He listened intently to my stories as well as to my grandmother's, so he came to know Hana's life almost as well as I did.

His immigration paperwork was in progress, and to sustain ourselves financially, we began hosting Airbnb guests in our spare bedroom. The school year was well underway, and I was teaching Hana's story in the classroom, continuing to freelance as a writer and photographer, and writing the first draft of this book. Sergiusz and I were both hustling, trying to make it in the gig economy and each working from home—me by choice and Sergiusz by necessity—as we waited for the government to grant him a work visa.

We fought sometimes, definitely more now that we were married. Our life felt more permanent in America. The stakes were raised. He struggled with the limitations put on him by the government, and I was lonely. I missed my grandmother. Even though I was still working with her story every day, being back in Boston put me at a distance from her life. Her story had become a weight of responsibility. How was I ever going to be able to write it into existence for people who hadn't been on the journey with me? No matter what words I put on paper, they felt inauthentic, forced, and never enough. She had been so dedicated to keeping her diary and documenting her world. She spent so much time reflecting on the mundane and recounting the quiet moments. None of her stories ever felt like they were finished—one narrative would just lead into another, and they never took a chronological path, as memories hardly ever do. I didn't know how I could communicate that to others. Did I even have a right to tell others? How could I honor all of it if I left any of it out? Sometimes I would find myself irrationally angry that Sergiusz wouldn't be able to fix this feeling. I was embarrassed when I broke down into uncontrollable tears and scared him with my panicked breathing.

Sergiusz did his best to peel back my layers of loneliness, but the truth is that I didn't know how to let him, and even though he was now with me every day, I felt like I missed him too. We had a queen-size mattress now, a big apartment, and a kitchen full of wedding gifts, yet I often felt nostalgic for our small studio in Warsaw. I missed the days when it was just me, him, and history.

Every few weeks, we tried to visit the Polish Triangle, a neighborhood in Boston full of Polish immigrants. There was a church where Sergiusz could vote in his nation's elections and a traditional Polish restaurant where we ate pierogies and drank Żywiec beer for five times the cost back in Poland. In a small European grocery store, we could find the mayonnaise, cheeses, and white fish he was used to eating at home. That is where we purchased all the ingredients necessary to host our first party as a married couple—a celebration of Poland's Independence Day, which comes in early November. We invited friends to drink vodka, eat sausages and all types of pickled things, and challenged them to say Polish words like *wstrzemięź-liwość* (restraint), *źdźbło* (blade, as in a blade of grass), *gżegżółka* (cuckoo, the bird), or the easier to pronounce *kurwa*, which Sergiusz (and now I) used regularly as a substitute for "fuck."

We gathered with my family for Sergiusz's first Thanksgiving feast in America, knowing that in future years this would be his holiday. He was an artist in the kitchen and couldn't wait to be the one who cooked the turkey. He enjoyed every bite of every meal he ate and every conversation with every new person he met. Sergiusz's curiosity gave him an unending amount of joy in everyday life, and he fit in with my family right away.

I can pinpoint exactly when I became a part of his family. It was during the Christmas season of 2014, a month or so before we officially became engaged. I road-tripped with Sergiusz and his parents from Poland, through Germany and Austria, to Folgarida, a ski resort in the province of Trento in the Italian Alps. He had grown up visiting this place; twelve-hour drives for annual ski trips with family friends were the norm.

We began our drive at dawn. I was both emotionally and physically exhausted, having spent the previous five weeks in Prague, and was nursing a persistent migraine as I sat in the back seat of their Land Rover. Sergiusz was next to me, his body positioned so both I and Kastor, his aging terrier, could use him as a pillow.

We spent the first night of that trip in Munich, where Aleksander, Sergiusz's father, took us on a beer hall tour throughout the city. One of our first stops was a pub rumored to be where Hitler once hung out. We sat with strangers around a long communal wooden table and slammed our thick steins together, allowing the foamy heads to spill over as we proclaimed, "*Prost!*" We visited Christmas markets, where we drank mulled wine as we browsed the display cases of cured meats and cheeses. Aleksander and Sergiusz ate heavy portions of sausage while I assured them I was fine with potato soup and sauerkraut. Sergiusz had never brought a girl home and most certainly never took one on vacation with his family. I was the first girl he ever said "I love you" to. Danuta, his mother, was still warming up to the idea that I wasn't Polish, predicting that our future would be complicated—a foot on each continent. His father was just pleased that his son had found someone. It was now the three of them and me.

When we arrived at our destination in Italy, we traveled by ski lift to the chalet (a word I only learned then). The wooden lodge was idyllic. When you walked in, there was a bar to the left and a restaurant straight ahead. Skiers walked in funny strides, balancing on their boots and lost in thick layers. The walls and the ceilings were wooden, radiating warmth against the snowy landscape. Outside the doors, Europeans who all looked alike but spoke in different languages—a vacation version of the Tower of Babel— sped past us to the bottom of the run. Inside, they ate first courses of pasta and warmed their stomachs with *bombardinos*, Italian eggnog cocktails.

When we checked in, the chalet owner, Frederico, who knew Sergiusz's family well, realized that when he booked the reservations, he had thought I was a man named Boston and not Sergiusz's girlfriend *from* Boston, so he had given us a room with two twin beds instead of a full. His parents promptly corrected the staff, proudly showing us off as a couple, and we were reassigned to a room with a bed we could share. In the process, there was discussion of my last name.

"Cerrotti? She speaks Italian, no?" asked Frederico.

In offbeat unison, we all said, "No. Yes, (she is / I am) Italian. But no, (she does not / I do not) speak Italian." For the duration of the trip, the staff charmingly referred to me as "Signora Boston, the Italian who speaks no Italian."

It was tradition for the Schellers to come to Folgarida with their extended group of friends, which now totaled about thirty Polish people and me. The days were for skiing, and the evenings for socializing. Every night, we ate dinner together—all thirty of us—in a reserved room. Each four-course meal began with a bowl of fresh pasta. I was the only person in the group who didn't speak Polish, the only non-European, the only one who didn't—and couldn't—ski, and the lone vegetarian.

I could communicate with Danuta, but she and I relied on Sergiusz to translate our conversations. If Sergiusz took too long to switch from one language to the other, she would turn to him and say, "*Przetłumacz to Rachael*" (translate for Rachael). Aleksander didn't speak much English, although I sensed he understood more than he let on. Even without a shared language, I knew that he was quite funny; I would sit back and listen as he and Sergiusz discussed everything from politics and sports to history, food, and travel. I knew Sergiusz well enough that I could tell the tone of conversation even when I didn't understand the language. I watched his hands move, waving away ideas he thought were ridiculous with a confident and sometimes cocky grin on his face. Sergiusz admired his father deeply and desperately wanted to be like him.

Aleksander was a strong man, both physically and in spirit. This was a second marriage for both him and Danuta. They began dating in 1983, and after communism fell, they built themselves a successful business, both working as engineers and in real estate. They worked hard, and they played hard. As a family, they taught me how to enjoy the fruits of my labor and the finer things in life. They admired their son and spoiled him, and now I was the recipient of that love as well.

Back in Boston, I would often have to remind Sergiusz that the life his father had built for himself hadn't happened overnight; success took time. But Sergiusz was impatient for the day he could provide for me the way his father provided for him. He was desperate to prove himself, to show every-one that he, too, could build something. I would often tell him, "Sergiusz, slow down. We always have tomorrow."

Sergiusz's immigration meant that for the first time, he wouldn't be able to spend the Christmas season with his family. We had made peace with this, as had his parents, and we had just seen them a couple months earlier when they came for our wedding, anyway.

One morning during that particularly warm December in 2015, I was in the kitchen preparing a late breakfast when Sergiusz received a phone call from his mother in Italy (a daily occurrence). I heard his voice in the hallway grow increasingly urgent as the conversation continued. I could pick up only what was said in repetition. I ran to him and found him with his back against the wall. He was repeating, "*Tata, Tata, Tata,*" and holding his thumb and index finger against his eyes to keep the tears from falling. Something had happened to his father.

I held him tightly around the waist. He moved the phone from his face and whispered, "My father had a stroke while skiing."

Danuta had found Aleksander facedown on the slopes. Just moments before, they had been happily skiing together. Now he was in a coma. Sergiusz translated fragments of information for me as he received them. We didn't know how severe the stroke was or what damage it had done to his brain or nervous system.

Sergiusz's back slid down the wall until he reached the floor, his body curled, his face hidden within his elbows. We knew he wasn't legally allowed to leave the country. We were still early in his immigration process, and he was locked in a jail cell of legal constraints. If he left the United States before having his paperwork approved, our case could be thrown out and he wouldn't be let back into the country.

We rushed to the immigration office in downtown Boston and sat in a quiet, sterile room that had multiple TVs airing the news on mute. I held his hand while he stared at his phone, desperate for a text from his mother saying everything was okay.

We put in a request to rush his travel permit and then had to make a decision: should he leave the United States to be with his parents and risk his case being thrown out? Or should he stay with me and risk not being there if his father died?

At his mother's urging, he stayed and we waited. First for one week, then another. The new year came and went. And every day we questioned whether he was doing the right thing by prioritizing being in America with me.

In January 2016, Sergiusz received an expedited travel permit from the United States Citizenship and Immigration Services, and with that came permission to work. His green card was the next step. That same month, his father was flown from Italy back to Poland, now in a medically induced coma. Danuta was by his side and reported to us that his recovery looked hopeful. Sergiusz finally flew home for a visit in March, and a collective sigh of relief was taken when Aleksander began to heal. We all looked forward to the summer, when we would be together in Denmark for our wedding celebration on Sine's farm.

There were no two people who influenced Sergiusz and me more in terms of our life plans than Sine and Torsten. They opened up a new world for us, and it was because of them that we began daydreaming about having our own farm, an idea that grew stronger for Sergiusz as he settled into life in New England. When he returned from visiting his parents in Poland that March of 2016, he made a career switch and found himself an apprenticeship on an organic farm in Massachusetts.

Every morning, he woke before the sun and spent the day planting and harvesting vegetables, sending me selfies of his face drenched with sweat and pictures of squashes, eggplants, garlic, herbs and bunches of sunflowers. He would return home with his fingernails caked with dirt and cucumbers in the pockets of his cargo pants. I had never known him to be so happy. I suggested that we move to Denmark, where I thought Sergiusz could work for Sine and Torsten. Since he was a European Union citizen, this wasn't an unrealistic idea. But Sergiusz was determined to become an American, so I didn't push too hard.

My family often joked that Sergiusz was the fastest-assimilating immigrant around. He proudly wore flannel shirts and a Boston Red Sox beanie and schooled himself in local Native American history. He would regularly take trips to Maine with my dad so he could learn how to take care of the family property. The two of them worked together during the day and sat by the wood stove at night talking about history, politics, farming, and theology. He was passionate about participating in his new democracy and marched at rallies alongside Bernie Sanders supporters, hoping to see the Polish Jewish democratic socialist candidate be voted into office. I followed behind him at these community events with my camera.

During the time Sergiusz and I were filing paperwork for his immigration, hundreds of thousands of people from the Middle East and Africa fled their homes and sought refuge in Europe. In 2015 alone—the peak year of what would become known as the European migrant crisis—more than a million migrants and refugees arrived in Europe by sea; an estimated four thousand drowned trying to make the crossing.

Denmark and Sweden were two of the most highly desired destinations among those fleeing the Middle East and Africa—especially Sweden, which with a population of just around ten million had a reputation for offering generous social services and the chance for family reunification. Some 35,000 of the 165,000 asylum seekers who arrived in Sweden in 2015 were unaccompanied refugee minors, children under the age of eighteen who had fled home without their parents—just like Hana. The number of displaced persons in the world climbed to a historically high level and, for the first time, surpassed records set in the aftermath of World War II. Governments and policy makers were trying to keep up, and public opinion thrashed on both sides—the isolationists and humanists yelled their opinions into the Internet. As my grandmother had said to me about her own displacement journey, "Everyone was trying to get somewhere, and no one wanted the people."

The whole world was on edge as the refugee crisis dominated the news, and leaders of the world's most powerful democracies were gaining power by capitalizing on fear and by espousing anti-immigrant rhetoric. Brexit was looming, as were the primaries for the American presidential election. More and more Swedes were voting for the Swedish Democrats, a political party with neo-Nazi roots. And a Danish right-wing government called the Danish People's Party was also gaining in the polls. In the Czech Republic, I had photographed citizens wearing buttons and holding signs during political rallies, stating, "Not my president!" about their leadership. Poland had already moved far to the right, away from their relatively new democratic ideals. Sergiusz would often tell Americans with a tone of embarrassment, "Poland already voted in their Trump." Sergiusz and I consumed European news and sports with intensity. When the Euro Cup was on, we would wake up early to stream the football games while wearing our bright red T-shirts that read *Polska*. Sergiusz would pick up the phone every time his team was about to score so he could cheer with his parents, who were watching from their couch in Poznań. From a political stance, the headlines and photographs from Europe began to echo the same dark themes that started my grandmother's story:

VIOLENCE HAS FORCED 60 MILLION
PEOPLE FROM THEIR HOMES.
(*The Atlantic*, June 17, 2015)

MIGRANTS ENTER DENMARK,
DETERMINED TO REACH SWEDEN.
(*National Public Radio*, September 10, 2015)

'NOW THEY CAN STOP RUNNING':
SWEDEN'S SHARP RISE IN CHILD REFUGEES.
(*The Guardian*, September 10, 2015)

HOW U.S. JOURNALISTS NORMALIZED THE RISE
OF HITLER AND MUSSOLINI.
(*Public Radio International*, December 13, 2016)

'NEVER FORGET,' THE WORLD SAID OF THE
HOLOCAUST. BUT THE WORLD IS FORGETTING.
(*Boston Globe*, May 1, 2016)

UNHCR REPORT: MORE DISPLACED
PERSONS NOW THAN AFTER WWII.
(*CNN*, June 20, 2016)

Statistics, photographs, articles, opinions—hateful, fearful, vengeful, and loving—tweets, posts, likes, links, and shares told of the horrors happening in our world, thousands of miles away as well as right next door. Photojournalists I knew traveled to Greece to photograph terrified migrants arriving by illegal and overcrowded boats; other photographers were sent to photograph the ones who didn't survive. Current events felt strange and cyclical, as though a new thread were being spun into the web of family stories I was retelling.

I returned to Europe that summer, leaving Sergiusz in Boston. We would spend a month away from each other, temporarily putting ourselves back into a long-distance relationship before he would join me for our wedding celebration. I knew that the politics of the past year had changed my grandmother's story. Current events were beginning to feel as relevant as the history books did.

I arrived in Denmark in late July and a few days later drove with Torsten from the farm to their summer cottage in southern Sweden, where Sine and the kids waited for us. We drove through Copenhagen to pick up his mom and then crossed the Øresund Bridge. I stared out over the water as we drove. Torsten's satellite radio played the public radio station in Maine as an homage to our time together in New England. Back when my grandmother had to cross this water to safety, there had been no bridge; now thousands of refugees and migrants were tying to get across it for the same reason she had boarded that boat in Denmark in 1943.

When we approached the Swedish side, border control was stopping each vehicle. Torsten rolled down his window, and a young officer strained his neck to look at me in the back seat. He motioned for my passport. I watched as he leafed through it with little curiosity. It was the first time while following my grandmother's story that I had to prove my identity in order to cross a border. But I wasn't someone he was trained to be worried about.

CHAPTER 14

THEY CAME BY BOAT

*When my children were leaving [the house] . . . I kept telling myself,
"How lucky I am." They were going voluntarily, to an adventure, and
often I mentioned to my children how lucky they were, as they always
knew, and still know, that there is a place to come back to. I never had
that. Once a door was closed, I didn't have the key.*

—HANA'S DIARY, 1986

During the summer, the Danish countryside was blanketed in violet, pale
pink, and light green hues. The sun rose early, and fog coated the flowers
with a thin layer of dew. The golden stalks of wheat fluttered like flags in
the soft and chilling wind. And when the sun finally did set, late in the
evening, the windmills and horses became silhouettes against the sky.

There had been a full circle of life since I last visited Sine and Torsten's
farm. Their two bulls had gone to slaughter, as had their pig. But the pig's
offspring were now part of the family, as was a whole new generation of
sheep, a couple of new horses, and two milking cows. And much to their
children's excitement, Sine and Torsten had adopted a Danish-Swedish
farm dog named Luka, who had a habit of stealing our shoes and hiding
them in the garden.

The children and I had become close, especially after spending time
together in Maine. They welcomed me back to Denmark with homemade

gifts. Liva was just a few months shy of becoming a teen, and Lauge's English was so good that we were now conversing in full sentences, but with Silje, I still needed the camera to communicate. She would pose. I would snap a picture and show it to her. She would laugh. I would smile and say to her, "*En til?*" (One more).

I reprised my role as house chef and tagged along with the family wherever they went, always with a couple of cameras around my neck. My intention that summer in 2016 was to straddle the roles of documentarian and do-it-yourself bride, but I had a hard time with the latter, feeling resentful whenever a wedding-related task took me away from my grandmother's story.

I spent some time in Copenhagen that summer as well, becoming closer with Dáša's descendants. I visited Bent Melchior again, the rabbi who had been on the same refugee boat as my grandmother. It had always felt comfortable with him, but now it felt natural. Time had turned him into the type of friend that I wouldn't dare not visit when in town. I was eager to hear his reflections on the refugee crisis. I wanted to know if current events were changing his memories the way they were changing my grandmother's memories for me.

"I left Europe last year in June," I first reminded him. "And within a couple of weeks of being back in the United States, all over the media were photographs, articles, and debatable opinions about the thousands and thousands of refugees arriving in Denmark and Sweden. They were talking about closing borders. And while the borders have remained open, there are now passport checks in places there weren't a year before. How does that make you feel?"

He sat back in his chair, pulling on the wire of the small microphone I had clipped to his shirt. "When the Second World War ended, we were extremely optimistic," he began to say. "That was still even before we heard the terrible things that happened in the camps, but we thought that mankind had suffered so much that they would understand that war was not the answer. I mean, we had lived to see miracles happen on the sea. And I think of these thousands of people who have tried to come over the Mediterranean today. I think this is a shame on our generation and of our time, that we let this catastrophe happen. I don't know how that should be forgiven. Because you can think of refugees in one way and another way, but here you have human beings dying. So forget whether they are right or they are wrong. To begin with, you have to save them."

I also went back to Sweden that summer to visit the Persson family—the descendants of the fisherman who rescued the refugee boat my grandmother and Bent were on in 1943. Annika, Per-Arne's daughter, offered to let me stay with her family and photograph a bit of their life.

It was a cool August evening when she took me back to her parents' house. A summer storm had subsided a few hours before we arrived. The light flowed into their home and softly highlighted the framed newspaper article on the wall that told of Per-Arne's lifelong friendship with Bent. It looked different to me now that my relationship with each of them had grown. It was personal. We shared this story. Next to the article, to my surprise, hung two framed photographs of my grandmother—one of Hana and me near the time of her death, and one of my grandmother as a teenager. I had given the pictures to Per-Arne and Marianne during my last visit. There was also a picture of me standing on the shore propped up on a table.

As it had been with Bent, we were more comfortable around each other now that we had a year and a half of friendship behind us. Marianne and I were even Facebook friends. The computer from where she followed my travels overlooked the seashore that had become famous in the retelling of my grandmother's journey. Annika once again did her best to translate the conversation, simplifying her father's stories to match her English vocabulary and often choosing to omit his dirty jokes.

I asked how they felt about the thousands of migrants coming into their country. They explained that much of the conversation happening in their country was a question of status. Was someone a refugee or a migrant? How could one tell? Who was in charge of deciding? And regardless, was there space for them to stay? Who should be granted asylum and who should be sent back home?

That evening, at my request, Annika and her husband brought me back to the former bed-and-breakfast where my grandmother had stayed her first night as a refugee in Sweden. I wanted to take more photos, not satisfied with what I had collected the year before. The house was only a couple of minutes down the road. They opted to wait in the car as I went to explore.

It looked vacant from the outside. The sign that faced the street and advertised guest rooms was crossed out with white paint. The grass was a healthy green, and the bushes were no longer skeletons of bare branches. Folding wooden chairs created a social space on a slice of the yard. I picked up my camera to snap a photograph as a teenage boy walked onto the wraparound balcony.

"No photos, no photos," I heard a woman say, urgently opening one of the ground-floor doors. I pulled the camera away from my eye and walked toward her, introducing myself in one quick breath. "Hi, my name is Rachael. I'm a journalist from Boston. My grandmother stayed here when she was a refugee in 1943, during the Holocaust. I am here working on a documentary project. And I am just wondering, Why can't I take pictures?"

She told me I couldn't take pictures because there were refugees living there now.

"Oh, okay. That is really interesting since my grandmother was here as a refugee almost seventy-five years ago. Would it be okay if I came in and saw the place?"

Without hesitation, she welcomed me into the group home. The walls were bare and the hallway was dark, speckled with only a little natural light. A few soccer balls were scattered around the place, and the communal areas looked lived in. I was told that only boys lived here now; all were between the ages of fourteen and eighteen. Most were from Afghanistan, Syria, and Somalia, and all had arrived without their parents. I was introduced to a few of them; some were cooking in the kitchen, while others watched TV. They were indifferent to my presence.

"Did most of these boys come by boat?" I asked as we walked from room to room.

The social worker logged the points of their journey for me, "Yes. Most at some point came across the Mediterranean and then from there up to

Germany. In Germany they boarded another boat—but a legal one—to take them here to Sweden."

"And is it okay if I take pictures of the house if nobody is in the photograph?" I asked. "For the story about my grandmother."

"Yes, that's fine. But please be careful. There have been some instances where houses like this have been burned down by people who don't want the refugees here."

The shores of Sweden never looked the same to me after meeting those boys. That night, while photographing the sunset, I watched the Swedish flag flap aggressively in the wind as I set my camera on a tripod and did a series of self-portraits. A lone bench was nearby, from when Per-Arne was still able to leave his house without assistance. The rain had stopped, but the moisture in the air remained, and the sunset now draped the coast with pinks and oranges and reds that faded into shades of light and dark blues with purple hues. The white caps of the sea created a stark contrast to the sky as nightfall came nearer. The reflection of war was back. Able-bodied youngsters, stripped of their homes, their families, and their childhoods, laid their heads to rest within the same walls as Hana once did. They ran from their countries with similar uncertainties, but said their prayers in a different language.

––––––––

A few weeks later, on a Saturday afternoon in late August 2016 in the Danish countryside, the sun was high in the sky, sending warm rays of tender energy to the people below. The air was so still that only the vibrations of voices could disturb the calm; each language spoken rippled over the landscape with a different tempo. The land was patterned with friends and family from faraway places like Poland, America, Mexico, England, Sweden, Germany, and of course, other parts of Denmark. Everyone had gathered in their dresses and suits to celebrate us, the bride and groom.

I walked out of the apartment I had come to call home and looked out at Sine and Torsten's farm. This was the place I now returned to between all my European travels, where my anxieties disappeared, where my grandmother's past most intimately intersected with my present.

"This connection," Sine once said. "It is strange. Because we are not related or anything. It's not blood, but it is another connection that is very important."

Jensine, Sine's grandmother, passed away when she was ninety-four. Hana passed away when she was eighty-five. Sine and I, along with Knud-Arne and other family members, had a recurring conversation about how wonderful it would have been if the two women had met in old age. Our friendship felt like the life that came after death. It was a friendship that made the history of the Holocaust feel gentler.

I was wearing a long flowing dress with a faint green floral design. Sine wore a fitted jumpsuit, her heels dug slightly into the grass beneath her.

"Are you ready?" she asked me.

"I think so," I replied. Sergiusz had already left the apartment and made his way to the event house. I had watched as he and his friends walked up the country road, thinking that they looked like illustrations in a child's fairytale.

"What would Jensine and Hana be saying?" I then said. "There is no way they would ever believe this—that my wedding celebration would be on your farm."

Sine laughed cozily. "I think our grandmothers are smiling down on us."

Sergiusz and I didn't walk down an aisle, but we had a small ceremony officiated by my father, who stood with my mother and Sergiusz's parents. We signed a *ketubah* as our community made a semicircle around us in the backyard. Sergiusz stepped on a glass, in accordance with Jewish tradition, and then, in a bow to Polish tradition, we both took a shot of vodka and threw the glasses over our shoulders. This was followed by the presentation of bread and salt—also a Polish tradition. "The bread is offered so that the couple may never know hunger," my father said, sharing what Danuta had taught him. "The salt symbolizes life's difficulties and the importance of learning how to cope." We then raised the Danish flag.

During the meal, the Danes brought out their traditions, clanking their cutlery against their plates, signaling for Sergiusz and me to stand on chairs and kiss in front of everyone. And then, they stomped their feet, prompting everyone else to join in, forcing us underneath a table to kiss, as Hana and Dáša had done when they were fourteen.

Sine, Torsten, and their children mingled with the Bergmanns, Dáša's descendants. Knud-Arne chatted with my aunts and uncle. Our American and German friends hung out with our Polish friends, American cousins with Polish cousins. We had a branch of my father's Danish family tree there as well, a family we became close with after discovering a shared grandfather from seven generations back.

Our plates were full of food, and our glasses overflowed. Sergiusz had prepared a delicious meal for seventy people. His arms were toned and tanned from his months working as a farmer, and his posture was that of a man who knew who he was and where he was going. He held a different identity than the year before when he had left Europe. He was now an American immigrant and a Polish emigrant. He was married, confident in our relationship, hopeful about what came next, and becoming content with himself.

"You know, after this party, we get to actually build this life for ourselves," he whispered to me as we posed for pictures, looking to the farmland that surrounded us. We were standing inside of our daydream.

"I would like to give a toast to Rachael and Sergiusz," my father began.

Sergiusz translated his words into Polish for our room full of guests as they ate.

"And to Danuta and Aleksander and all of your family."

"*Za Danutę i Aleksandra oraz całą waszą rodzinę.*"

"And to all of the wonderful and great things that are going to happen in the future and for the bonds that are made here together."

"*Za wszystkie wspaniałe chwile, które wydarzą się w przyszłości oraz za więzi, które razem tutaj zawarliśmy.*"

"And for the love that brings us together."

"*Za miłość, która zbliża nas do siebie.*"

"And I would also like to say to Sergiusz, . . ."

"*I jeszcze chciałbym dodać* . . . to me, . . ."

"You can borrow my car anytime."

Around 11:00 p.m., the cake was cut and the tables and chairs were pushed aside so the dancing could begin. I wrapped my arms around my husband's neck as he took hold of my waist, and our community danced in a circle around us, steadfast in their support of our relationship. The acceptance came in Danish and Swedish and English, in German and in Polish. It came from the urban and the rural corners of our worlds, from the old and the young, the sick and the healthy. It came from the Jews and the Lutherans and Catholics, who found amusement and amazement in the many cultures we felt to be our own. Generations before, the world had told our grandparents to run from each other, and yet here we were.

CHAPTER 15

ONLY A FOOL
WOULDN'T BE SCARED

My story is an uplifting one.

—HANA DUBOVÁ, 2001

A couple of weeks after the wedding party, once back in Boston, Sergiusz turned to me while making dinner and said, "I never asked you. How do you feel now that the party is over?"

This question was a bit surprising as we had been swooning over the celebration since we got home. "It was amazing," I said. "Honestly, it feels like a dream. How did we pull that off?"

"I feel like I proved myself," he stated as if he had been waiting to say this out loud his entire life. "It's like I can sit back and relax now. Everyone understands."

He was referring to his unconventional path. In his community, he was always the exception. He found homes abroad and comfort within so many languages that were not his own. When we walked around Boston, he would eavesdrop on every conversation—English, Hebrew, Russian. Although raised Catholic, he knew more about Judaism than most. Like me, he loved immersing himself in unfamiliar ways of life. He studied for a career in politics yet was working as an organic farmer. And although he was the guy who had never had a serious girlfriend, he was among the first of his friends to get married—and to an American, for that matter. When in Poland, he felt too international. When in Israel, he felt too Polish. When in America, he felt like an immigrant. But with me, he was good, and now everyone understood why.

"Proved yourself?" I said with inquisitive enthusiasm. "No way. This is permission to *start* proving ourselves."

Sergiusz and I balanced each other this way. We took turns being present in the moment and focused on the future. We challenged each other, sometimes in very frustrating, albeit supportive, ways.

We were in a new routine as Sergiusz had injured himself a few weeks after returning to his work on the farm in Massachusetts. We were both back to working from home. One morning, after saying goodbye to our Airbnb guest, we moved a spare desk from the office into our bedroom so he could have his own space. He started meticulously organizing his papers, stacking them by categories: work, immigration, education. He balanced his search for freelance writing and translation gigs with running into the office where I was working to chat my ear off about properties in Maine he wanted to buy. We had a map on the wall that he was marking up with potential new homes. I could hear the growing excitement in his voice: "We could have a farm here, and here, and here," he kept saying.

"Sergiusz," I scolded him playfully, "you gotta let me work."

"Okay, okay," he responded, flashing his dimples.

"Give me like an hour, and we can cook dinner," I said, giving in to him.

A few minutes later, around 5:00 p.m., Sergiusz sent an email to me and my father with the subject line "It's Good to Dream Sometimes." In it was a link to a stunning gentleman's farm in Maine. I checked it out and went back to editing photos.

I had thousands and thousands of pictures to sort through. Over the years, my grandmother's archive had grown to be so big that it felt impossible to wade through. Each new trip I took added to it. I was recording most of my conversations with both video and audio, and I never went anywhere without at least two cameras. Interviews became transcripts. Individual pictures became collections. Ticket stubs, receipts, printouts of directions, pamphlets from museums, and other saved scraps of paper filled boxes. My job, at least from my photographer's perspective, was to now take the simple, quiet images of the places I'd been and layer in the history. The task excited me. It made everything meaningful.

A loud crash took me out of my rabbit hole of history.

"Sergiusz?" I yelled. "What was that?"

No response.

"Sergiusz?"

No response. So I got up, untangling my legs from the wires of hard drives and chargers and walked across the hallway to our bedroom. "Sergiusz?" I said again, quieter this time.

I didn't see him until I peered around the bed. He was on the floor, his body crumpled.

"Sergiusz?" I asked again, panicked. I thought maybe he had tipped backward in his chair and was shocked or embarrassed.

No response.

"Sergiusz?" I moved fast, bending down to shake him. "Sergiusz? Sergiusz? Sergiusz!"

No response. I looked at his face and saw it struggling.

"SERGIUSZ! SERGIUSZ! SERGIUSZ!"

I ran for his phone, my socks slipping on the hardwood floor. I dialed 911. The ringtone went through the portable speakers. Then it disconnected. I ran for my phone, which was in the office, and called again as I ran back across the hallway to his body. I looked at his eyes. I looked at his face. He was still with me. He could see me. I know it.

"Hello, hello," I heaved into the phone. "My husband. I don't know. He just collapsed. Yes, I am practicing CPR. Okay. I'm continuing. Yes, I'll stay on the phone. Second floor. Tremont Street. Oak Square. Oh my God. Sergiusz. Sergiusz. Yes. Yes, I'm here. Sergiusz. Please . . ."

When I gave him CPR, I could feel him feel me. I knew his body knew me. I wanted his body, and his body wanted me. I loved him, and he loved me. I kept breathing into him, wanting to caress him gently but instead forced my body on top of his as I did compression after compression.

Twelve uniformed men arrived at the apartment—EMTs, police officers, firefighters, a detective. They ordered me away from his body. I know that is the moment his eyes stopped seeing me; they left him when I moved away. His body became empty. "Is he on drugs?" one asked me.

"No!" I cried, jumping from one side of the bed to another, gathering his green card and passport.

An EMT ripped off his T-shirt. It was his light blue one that depicted a cartoon sloth parachuting through the sky. They pulled him to a different part of the bedroom floor where they had more space to work and talked with each other as if I wasn't there. "He is turning blue," one of them said.

"I know what that means!" I gasped. The sound on the portable heart monitor went flat. I yelled, "I have seen the movies. I know what that sound means." They didn't respond, but rather turned off the machine.

At the hospital, I watched dozens of medical professionals stand around him. They removed his remaining clothes in order to attach bags of fluids to his body. They did everything they could to bring him back to life. With each electric shock, I thought they would heal his heart. They let me speak to him. "Please, Sergiusz," I remember saying. "Please don't leave me. I love you. *Kocham Cię, Moje Serce.* I love you. Please, please, don't leave me. *Ani ohevet otcha.* Just wake up. Come back home."

My mom was there at the hospital with me, as were our friends Emily and Jasmine. We had been in a group chat with them when he collapsed. Our rabbi also came; my mom had called him immediately. He sang a *nigun*, a Hebrew melody that brought comfort as my knees buckled and I fell to the floor.

———

Sergiusz was pronounced dead at 7:34 p.m. on September 29, 2016. He died from an undiagnosed heart disease. Calling his parents in the middle of the night to tell them that their son had died is the hardest thing I have ever had to do.

I replay the scene of his death in my head over and over. It does not discriminate where or when it haunts me. Sometimes I'll be reaching for milk at the grocery store or turning down a street or staring at a beautiful tree, and I'll see his eyes roll back inside his head. And every time I hear a loud thud, my body tightens and my heart races. It is a deafening fear that I now have that someone, anyone, or everyone will die in front of me.

In the days and weeks after Sergiusz died, when the flashbacks were persistent and all-consuming, I'd touch his wedding ring, which I now wore around my neck, and would feel imprisoned by the memory of caressing his corpse. It was like I was addicted to the attire of his death. I longed for the feeling of his body, wishing I could touch it once more. I thought often about the nurse who I'd asked to pull the wedding band from his finger. I told her I was too scared to hurt him. I was consumed by guilt. I desperately tried to save his life, but what if I had done the CPR wrong? What if he had called for me and I hadn't heard him? What if I hadn't pushed him out of the office? Would he still be here if I had given him more of my time?

I was haunted by the memory of sitting by his deathbed. I remember thinking about my grandmother and hating myself for it. In those early minutes of loss, I stared at my husband's dimples, not believing that I would never see him smile again. I felt like a fraud and a fool. How could I have thought that I could narrate my grandmother's story of grief? I'd spent so many years telling people that Hana's story was uplifting because she survived. "She never witnessed death," I would say almost as if it were a badge of good mental health.

I learned this perspective from her. When she told me her story, she didn't traumatize me with any of the dark details. I had to go out and research those on my own. Looking back, I don't really think it was even a story of grief that she told me. It was an adventure—a sad story with a happy ending that included a granddaughter spending quality time with her grandmother. She told me the unexpected plots and heroic twists. The whole narrative was wrapped in the gift that she called life. Perhaps the perspective of adventure protected her. It certainly protected me.

In 1990 she wrote in her diary about speaking to students about her experience in the Holocaust:

> *Since my story is unique, since I have not been in a concentration camp, since I have had to struggle to survive on my own, I talk about relying on oneself. [I talk] about tenacity, about loneliness, about*

feeling [like] an outcast, a stranger, about the drive to study, to learn to be somebody without support either from a group or an individual. All alone. This I feel and think hits much more home for this inner self than talking about hardship.

What quiets the inner scolding of my loss is the memory of the morning after, when I awoke in my parent's basement as a twenty-seven-year-old widow. My mom was laying next to me, her eyes wide. I looked out the window. The sky was beautiful—uncomfortably so. The sun was shining through the foliage, which was just beginning to change from summer greens to fall oranges and reds. As I turned my head a bit in either direction, the rays of light shifted in shape and vibrancy, illuminating different leaves. With just the slightest movement, my perspective changed.

My grandmother was once asked in an interview how her wartime experience influenced her life. "I cannot tell you that, because I do not know how my life would have been without it," she responded. "The question I cannot answer. I don't know how it would have been. I don't know what would have become of me. I don't know whether I would have an education. I don't know. I don't know. I don't know."

This is how I feel. I have no idea what would have been of my grandmother's memory and of my own story had Sergiusz not died.

I never slept in my apartment again. In our bedroom, where his heart had stopped, was an unmade bed, the sheets strewn about from my frantic movements trying to collect his forms of identification. His wide-brimmed hat, which he took every day to the farm, hung on the wall next to my fedora, which I most often wore when we were kicking back on the porch. A few framed photographs from our ceremony in Maine sat on our dressers; we had yet to receive the photographs from our celebration in Denmark. Bottles of nail polish, stacks of unread books, and piles of dirty laundry created a still-life in the room.

The office had also been left as it was when I first heard him collapse. Hard drives sat next to my computer, holding the images of our relationship and every word that my grandmother had written about her life and her loss. My yoga mat was rolled up in the corner, and his bike leaned up against the wall. The closet in the office was stuffed full of our clothes. His flannel shirts hung next to mine, his suits next to my dresses. His stacks upon stacks of graphic tees were ironed and folded neatly in his drawers.

Our kitchen was his sanctuary, where his artistry came alive. Sergiusz spent far too much money on groceries, buying organic, locally sourced foods. When we registered for wedding gifts, so much of what we asked for was for the kitchen—a French press for coffee, a charming tea pot, a beautiful set of blue ceramic dishes, a decanter for whiskey, and a stovetop grill. The few possessions he brought with him to Boston included a shredder for parmesan cheese, which his parents had bought him as a birthday gift in Tuscany, and a cast-iron frying pan that required two hands for me to lift it from the stove to the sink.

Hanging above our dining room table was a framed menu from one of the restaurants we visited in Italy with his family. In every room of our home were artifacts from our travels—the delicate espresso cup he gave me when we first started dating, the Matisyahu poster that we innocently stole from a city wall back when we were college kids living in Jerusalem, and dozens of vinyl records we had collected together.

The papers and emails from our life looked different now, every little note, every apology, and confession of love read differently now. I treasured every piece of paper that held Sergiusz's handwritings. It all inadvertently became a part of the archive.

I sorted through our digital love notes as well. Sergiusz didn't write much, but there was one email he wrote in 2014 when I was in Prague that remains in my inbox to this day:

November 24, 2014

Dear Rachael,

I promised you an email and sitting down to write to you as I just made myself a Bloody Mary seems like a hard task. What should I write to you about? I tell you (almost) everything that goes through my mind, you can read me like an open book; we talk every day, and we communicate so well that there's very little left unsaid or unfelt. Yet, now that I have started thinking about it, there are plenty of things and thoughts I want to share with you. For starters, I love you. You've heard me say it a dozen times a day and we never miss an opportunity to say 'I love you' to each other. I told you words can't express what I feel for you and it's true. It's a huge balagan of different feelings for you that I can't call anything else but love. When I see you, I smile. When I touch you, I feel home. When you look at me with your ocean-deep mesmerizing eyes, I just can't look away. It feels too good to look at you. I have never cared for anyone as I do for you; I have never entrusted my life to anyone but you, and I have never felt so comfortable about myself as I am with you. We said at the very beginning of our love that we want to spend our lives together. The more we are together, the more I believe (know?) that it is the only way I can be happy and fulfilled in life. That a life without you will be just a lonely, empty existence. You fill me up with energy to act and go forward.

I have my fears about our future which stem mostly from my own self-doubt. I ask myself if I am strong and good enough of a person to spend the rest of my life with you. If I will be always good to you and make you happy. If I give up on life at some point. If bad luck and circumstances will tear us apart. If we succeed at living the life we want for ourselves. Some say that in order to love someone, you first must love yourself. Will I always be at peace with who I am and what I do? And if not, will you get hurt because of it?

But only a fool wouldn't be scared. Fear is there to be felt and controlled, because that is what makes people stronger. These fears, these doubts are overpowered by my confidence in us, because I know I can't live without you. If I fall on the way, you will pick me up and carry me and I will do the same for you. You are the most loyal friend I ever had and it's a huge part of why I love you. I trust you indefinitely with anything. The best evidence of that is the fact that I fall asleep next to you feeling like the safest person in the world. This too, is definitely one of the strongest feelings I have for you.

I want to write about our friendship. Love and friendship are close, but love is a superior feeling; it's not something you can get rid of or cease. I have never believed people who say they don't love someone anymore. To me, it means they never loved that certain someone. When it comes to us, love is something I will always feel for you no matter what the future brings our way. I will swear by it anytime, anywhere. Love does not equal liking each other though. Love and hate can be two complimentary feelings. Love can hurt and be destructive. Yet friendship in love is something way more unique and serene than "just" love. The fact that we are friends, not just good friends, but best, loving friends is a source of insurmountable happiness and joy for me. I can't verbalize it accurately enough—we share the likes and dislikes, we think alike and about each other, we care for each other before anything else, we laugh more than we argue, we need each other's presence to flourish. It was way easier to make a decision to come live with you in your hometown because of that and frankly speaking I didn't even think about it for too long. What could be better for me than living with a best friend whom I love and cherish, care for and have fun with? Obviously, the fact that you live in Boston, Massachusetts, not Bosnia or Morocco, made a huge difference. But hypothetical questions like "what if?" are not the way to think about these issues. I am simply thankful that things that are beyond our control turn out to be in our favor. There could have been way more obstacles on our path to be together.

I want to say so much more, but words are vain and actions prove the actual intentions. I will follow you anywhere and stick to you no matter what life hurls at us and I hope you will do the same for me. I know you're the one.

Love,
Sergio

Sine came to the funeral. She was one of the first people I called after Sergiusz died. She and Lauge flew to Boston nearly immediately. I will never forget seeing Lauge's face when he greeted me at the synagogue on the morning of the service. It was such raw sadness. Just a month before, he and Sergiusz were building a birdhouse in their backyard on the farm. Lauge sobbed as he wrapped his eleven-year-old arms around my waist. Sine and I fell apart when we saw each other. She handed me flowers from their farm.

The first time I stood at the head of a sanctuary full of people was when I was twelve years old and had my bat mitzvah. I had chubby cheeks and braces, and my hair was pulled back into a French braid that I thought made me look like a boy. I wore a short, dark blue dress adorned with subtle beadwork where the fabric hit my upper thigh. The September 11 attacks on the World Trade Center had happened just a month and a half before, and I had recently lost two friends in a school bus accident. Those losses were my first introduction to what it meant to die suddenly and too young.

A tradition of the bat mitzvah (or bar mitzvah, if you are a boy) is for the young person to read from the Torah, and I, a persistent child, insisted there was only one story from the entire year's worth of them I would read: the story of L'ech L'echa.

L'ech L'echa is found in the book of Genesis and literally translates to "go forth." God says to Abraham, "Go forth from your homeland to the land that I shall show you. I will make of you a great nation and I will bless you and make your name great." Abraham is seventy-five years old at the time, but he, his wife Sarah, and his brother's son take all of their possessions and leave for Canaan—the ancient land of Israel. There is more to the story—famine, infidelity, old age, jealousy—but I didn't care. I just wanted to know about the journey, about going forth, about the search for home.

The next time I stood alone at the front of a sanctuary full of people was when I spoke at my grandmother's funeral. I was wearing a short dress then as well, a green one that I thought she would approve of. I remember that day as a happy one, a celebration of life, joyful like she had been.

Sergiusz's parents and I decided that he would have two funerals—one at the synagogue in Boston, where I had grown up, and one at his parent's church in Poland, where Sergiusz had grown up. Those of us who felt his absence the most found some solace and humor in the fact that only Sergiusz could pull off a multilingual, international, and interfaith death. My rabbi told us that the immediate family wasn't expected to speak at the service, but all of us chose to—my parents, my brother, Sergiusz's parents, and me. In the days before the funeral, I listened as Aleksander sat in my parent's bedroom and practiced his speech. A family member in Poland had translated it into English for him.

I sat in a short dress again (black this time), in the front pew of the same synagogue where my bat mitzvah had taken place. The familiar sounds of Jewish song hung like a cloud over the congregation; I could feel the pairs of eyes staring at me before quietly averting themselves. When I closed my eyes, I watched my husband die again and again.

Sergiusz's parents sat on one side of me and my parents on the other. Across the aisle was the priest my rabbi had asked to come so he could bring comfort and familiarity for Danuta and Aleksander. Sitting behind me were my aunts, uncles, cousins, and friends. For many of them, the wedding celebration was the last time they ever saw Sergiusz. Many others never even had a chance to meet him. We all thought there would be more time.

My fingers circled my palms as each member of my family spoke. I thought back to my childhood, when my grandmother would take my palm and circle it with her forefinger so slowly that it tickled. "Life will give you callouses," she would say to me. "But with each one, your skin becomes thicker."

When it was my turn to speak, my mother took my hand and held me steady as I walked to the bimah. Each step was thoughtful and slow. I stared out at the congregation with despair and authority as I unfolded a worn piece of paper. "I didn't write anything for today," I spoke into the crowd. "But I was going through the drawers next to Sergiusz's bed and found this letter I wrote for him last year on Thanksgiving. So I just thought I would read that."

My mother stepped back to give me some space but stayed by my side as I read:

So for this I am thankful. I am thankful for clarity and the ability to pave my own path. I am thankful for a loving husband. I am thankful for my body. I am thankful for my friends and my family. I am thankful that every day I wake up and am embraced by a man who loves me more than anyone else in this world. And I am thankful that I have the privilege of loving him as much as he loves me. I am thankful for my cozy apartment which has become our home. I am thankful for my in-laws who are the best family I could have asked for. I am thankful for all of my adventures over the past year, both those I experienced alone, deep in reflection and observation, and for those I experienced with company. I am thankful for the bits of language I have picked up along the way, humbling me at each letter, knowing that there is so much to the world that I don't understand and never will. I am thankful for Sushi (my dog) because every time I look at her, my whole world becomes a bit brighter and full of love. She makes everything better and gives me perspective. I am thankful for the recovery process—both physical and mental—because it keeps me confident that anything that is hurting right now will heal and become stronger. I am thankful for the books I read that take me to faraway places and remind me that the narrative I hold is just one of many. I am thankful for the music that centers me. And I am thankful for our record player and for not having a TV. I am thankful for the food that Sergiusz cooks me as it is much better than anything I cook for myself. I am thankful that he is healthy and that his mind is brilliant because one day I will give birth to his child. Knowing that his genes will be passed down and under his influence a new person will grow is the only reason I feel comfortable saying that I want children. It is because of who he is that I want to bring another person into this world. I am thankful that he loves my family and that they love him. I am thankful for our wedding. It was the most perfect day of my life, even if I had to sniffle the whole way through. I am thankful that the sewage tank got clogged, as the men of the family truly bonded over that experience. The broken things in life we must fix are what bring us together, or at least are what can bring us together if we let them. I am thankful that my parents support us, as do his. Their generosity makes me want to be the best and most authentic version of myself. I am thankful for this moment right now as all of the burdens I have been feeling and the weight of what life is has been taken away, even if just for today. We are incredibly lucky. If we want to move, we can. If we want to create, we can. If we want to sleep, to eat, to run, to play, to love, and to live, we can.

Ashes are much heavier than one would think, and you can see little pieces of bone among them. A few days after the funeral, my mom drove me, Danuta, and Aleksander to the cemetery to bring Sergiusz home. I never felt more like a wife than I did after becoming a widow. I signed more papers about his death than about our marriage. One signature on one document bound us for life, but it took dozens more to sort through his death. The black shoes I bought for the funeral clacked on the pavement as I walked from the parking lot, past the flower beds and urn options, to the building where the crematorium was. I handed over my license and said, "I am here to pick up Sergio, spelled S-E-R-G-I-U-S-Z, Scheller." I told them there should be two boxes. We requested his ashes be split in half so his parents could take him back to Poland. They handed my husband to me, and I carried him back to the car. I sat in the front seat with him on my lap as my mother drove the four of us back to her home in silence. A few days later, I watched Danuta walk out of my parents' house to their car. In the trunk was a plastic bag that held the clothes Sergiusz was wearing when he died. They had been cut up by the medics, nurses, and doctors. I watched from the window as she opened the bag and pressed her face into his clothes and wept.

It was adrenaline, fueled by bottles of bourbon and incessant dark humor, that got me through packing up what was left of our life so quickly. In another story, one with a more predictable ending, it would have taken months to organize our belongings into labeled boxes. I wouldn't have purged our furniture, desperately finding strangers who would take it for free. Our bed, lamps, desks, and extra chairs—everything had to go. I didn't want any of it anymore.

I accumulated twice as many condolence cards as wedding cards during those weeks spent dismantling my newly created life. (The two boxes still sit next to each other, collecting dust.) Most of the stuff I decided to keep was put into a five-by-five-foot storage unit on the side of a main road. The rest came with me to my parents' house. They welcomed me to stay in their basement for as long as I needed. I covered the temporary space with remnants of past lives—my grandmother's life, Sergiusz's life, and my own.

The lens through which I saw everything changed. When the 2016 US elections took place about a month and a half after Sergiusz died, I remember sitting on the floor in my parents' basement, painting my nails black as I watched the states turn red. "Reality is temporary," I whispered to myself, feeling uncomfortably grateful that Sergiusz didn't have to witness the disappointment of democracy. The results were officially announced on November 9—the anniversary of Kristallnacht. A man rumored to sleep with a book of Hitler's collected speeches near his bed was to become president. My head swelled with symbolism.

I returned to Europe soon after that, determined to retrace my own route following my grandmother's story. I felt I had no choice but to repeat my pursuit of her memory, this time bringing grief with me as a narrator. I thought that if I could step outside myself just enough to see my own story the way I saw my grandmother's, then I would be okay.

Back in Poland, I looked at Sergiusz's parents differently. As I watched them mourn their son, I imagined the pain and the agony that my great-grandparents must have felt sending Hana into the unknown. Together, Danuta, Aleksander, and I mimicked normalcy, even though we knew nothing would ever be the same. We celebrated Christmas together (my parents and brother even joined us in Poland), Danuta came shopping with me for new clothes, and we visited Sergiusz's grave. His room became my room. Danuta decorated it with holiday lights and plates of gingerbread cookies as she would have done if both of us were there. The bed was made as if we both were coming home. His American flag still hung on the wall. Over and over Danuta assured me I was still her daughter. She promised it would always feel that way. We talked late into the night over bottles of wine and fancy cheese. With nothing else to hold onto, we clutched onto tradition, even if it wasn't our own.

One night, she said to me, "I remember when Sergiusz began university and went to London; and then when he decided to go study in Israel, my mother would say to me, 'How could you let your son leave? How could you allow him to be so far from you?' And I always told her that I didn't have Sergiusz for myself. I had him so he could live his life, not accompany me through mine. And when he moved to America to be with you, I told him not to worry about being so far away from us. I told him, 'We share the same sky. We look at the same stars. So we are close.'"

My relationships in Denmark changed as well. Sine and I continued to grow closer. "I wasn't sure if you would want to come back," Sine told me. "Because of all the memories here." I told her that the farm was the only place that made sense to me. The memories were keeping me safe.

"I was thinking," she said. "I have friends from when I started school who are still my friends now, so it has been a lifelong friendship. We have lost also. It is thirty-five years maybe we have known each other, and we have lost parents and other people, but it is the normal life and the normal grief, and it is hard, and it is sad and everything, but you know it is going to happen. But this, this is just so wild—to have this experience with a stranger. I can't describe it with words because of course you changed a lot. You are still the same person, but of course a lot of things changed, and the whole story also changed. It puts the whole history in another perspective."

I began to experience the country where my grandmother found physical refuge as a place where I found emotional refuge. There was space on the farm for my anxiety to breathe, and therefore my inner demons mostly left me alone. I found satisfaction doing work I could measure. The familiarity of the farm kept me calm. The routine of cooking dinner for the family kept me feeling centered. I found comfort in being with the kids and loved living in a place where the sounds of a trampoline and children's laughter signified the end of a school day. I looked forward to hearing my footsteps walk up the grated metal staircase that led to my apartment, to my own cozy room that comforted me and soothed me.

I had never felt closer to Hana, but also hated myself for this feeling. I kept thinking to myself, now it's me who is the displaced girl in my story. The comparison was laden with guilt. Everything about grief was coated in guilt. It was nauseating to suddenly see myself in my grandmother's shoes. There was no war in my reality. No one did wrong. Six million didn't die—only one.

I thought of my grandmother and her parents. I thought of all the books about genocide I had studied and the current refugee crisis I was now telling stories about. I read and reread Hana's diaries, attaching meaning to what in past years I had paid no attention to. Every word she wrote read differently now, and sometimes it felt like she had written them just for me. I found some solace in the fact that she also played a game of emotional warfare with herself. Her diaries are full of self-criticism and contradiction—the repeated question of "Why was it I who survived?" She would tell herself the story she needed to hear, as we all do. I tried to use this fact as a source of kindness to myself, and sometimes it worked.

There was one piece of writing that spoke to me most during these early days of grief. It was from an essay she wrote in 2004 entitled "Vulnerability":

It is wise and best not to think about our vulnerability too much. It could lead to despair. It is far better to think about our strengths. Pretend we are wearing a soft tailor-made suit of armor. Nothing can pierce it as we go forth like one of King Arthur's knights. It's hard to do that. You have to put up a good front, a stiff upper lip. If our armor is made right, we can bend a little. Stoop down to pet a dog or pick a flower. It's hard to cook in it, or do housework. But it is best to keep it on at all times, especially at special occasion times like Christmas and birthdays, so you don't start thinking sad thoughts of the past. And it's good to have it on at wakes and funerals and other sad times . . . because you know every living person on the planet, and all animals too, are so very vulnerable to just about every horrible, awful, scary, terrifying, wonderful, loving, happy, pleasurable thing on Mother Earth, and that there is very little you can do to dodge it except plow right through and hope to avoid the bad and enjoy the good.

The guilt also came when I felt happy. That was harder to reckon with, especially when it overtook my fleeting feelings of hope, appreciation, and excitement. When I began to look at men again and imagine what it would be like to be with them, I felt like I was betraying Sergiusz's memory. Or, when music came back into my life, which was about six months after he died, I remember feeling that I had never known such intense beauty. I would play the same songs over and over again, staring at the ceiling with a blank face, but feeling like I was weeping inside.

"It's a strange way of feeling alive," Sine once said to me, referring to her father's death. "And you are not supposed to feel alive because somebody died. It was so crazy—I was so sad, and then in another way, I felt so alive every time I heard a song or saw the sunset and the birds and everything. It was so 'Aaaah, I could scream in the car.' It was so 'Aaaah, shit, I feel alive, but I am crying together with screaming.'"

Sine made me feel secure in my grief, like everything I was feeling was normal. If I stayed in my apartment for three days and didn't see anyone, it was fine. If I spent hours in their house, it was fine. Sine's farm comforted me. It was transforming. Here I would walk and take pictures, and sometimes I didn't miss anything. Of course it was not perfect, but when I came here, it felt like home, so trustful and open. I don't have any other word than *home*.

In the third week of January 2017, just days before my twenty-eighth birthday, I found myself sitting in a comfy chair in a warm living room in Southern Sweden with my feet curled up beneath me. Two thirteen-year-old boys, named Hadi and Mahdi, sat beside me; their necks were bent, their eyes focused on whatever was happening on their phones. Sitting on the couch across from me was an older gentleman from Iraq named Ghazi; he was resting after preparing a delicious meal for all of us, while his wife, Annika (who was Swedish), cleaned up in the kitchen. Annika is the one who invited me into their home. I met her, and Hadi and Mahdi, the previous September, a few days after the wedding party in Denmark. Sergiusz was with me that day, eager to be a part of my reporting trip.

Hadi and Mahdi were from Afghanistan and at age eleven had arrived in Sweden during the height of the mass migration that brought over a million migrants from the Middle East and Africa to Europe. Since meeting the refugees living in the house in Sweden where my grandmother stayed, I had been shifting some of my storytelling to focus on contemporary stories of young people seeking refuge in Scandinavia. Annika had voluntarily become a legal guardian, known in Sweden as a "*god man*" (good man), for Hadi and Mahdi. In a culture where some guardians take advantage of the system, Annika loved the boys like her own grandchildren. She integrated them into her family and was in a legal battle with the Swedish government to bring their mother and sisters from Iran, where they were living after fleeing Afghanistan. She was fighting for their family to be reunited. She reminded me of a modern-day Jensine.

That evening we were all watching the inauguration of Donald Trump as the president of the United States. Annika kept handing me photo albums. Some had pictures of when she and Ghazi lived in Baghdad, others when they lived in America. Some of the albums had their two sons in them as college students, and some albums had pictures of their sons as parents with children of their own. I flipped the pages, keeping my eyes averted from the television, and reluctantly engaged in a conversation about politics. The Europeans I knew didn't fear the new presidency the way I did. I tried to push away the frustration and the warning signs of what all these years of studying history had taught me. I looked toward Hadi and

Mahdi, resisting the urge to pick up my camera. I wanted to document their uninterest, thinking that just maybe it was similar to what the teens fleeing Czechoslovakia with my grandmother had felt, but decided not to disrupt their moment of calm. A week later, on January 27, 2017—which is International Holocaust Remembrance Day, the anniversary of the liberation of Auschwitz, and somewhat ironically, also my birthday—Donald Trump signed an "Executive Order Protecting the Nation from Foreign Terrorist Entry" into the United States. It would be the first of many such orders designed to bar "undesirable" immigrants from entering the country.

Since politics and grief had changed so much of how I experienced my grandmother's story, I decided to once again retrace my grandmother's train ride across America. It was now May 2017, and as I traveled, I also started a portrait series about young widowhood. I was determined to create community from my new aloneness and to make sense of my new memories. Hana's words became the backbone of the conversations I had with my fellow widows. I drew upon her strategies of living with trauma—stay busy; stay active; tell your story often, but know when to keep it to yourself. Her story taught me that there was no shame in telling a little white lie now and then.

I learned to deal with strange looks when people heard my story for the first time—the head tilt, the refrains of "I'm so sorry" and "You're so strong." I got used to platitudes and to people responding to my confession of widowhood with their own stories of loss; countless traumatic memories were casually told to me in bus depots and train stations. And I grew skilled at keeping my mouth shut—like the time I got out of an Uber with my heavy luggage and the driver said, "Geez, honey, what do you have in that bag? Your dead husband?" I knew the poor woman had no idea. In her head, I was just a young person traveling, so I let it go. It was easier to subscribe to her reality than to weigh her down with mine.

I often thought about a few lines my grandmother had written in that letter to her friend Lili: "On the train to Denver, I met in the dining car a gentleman who struck up a conversation with me. I was rather glad to be able to talk to someone, but told him a lie. I said that I am going to visit my family on the West Coast as he might have thought it quite odd if I told him the truth." I wished I had thought to ask my grandmother how often she chose to keep her story to herself for the sake of others. I wanted so badly to ask how hard it was to lie, to pretend that her past was gentle.

On the train ride across the United States, I stared out the window, watching the reflection of my ponytail as it overlapped the shapes of strangers sitting nearby. In the wake of grief, everything looked different. Everything felt different. The trees were greener. The nighttime sky was darker. The midnight kisses I witnessed on train station platforms lingered longer. The sunrises looked brighter. The music that provided the soundtrack for my ride felt spiritual. It was as if up until this point, my ability to understand the emotions hidden within my grandmother's writings had been limited. It didn't matter if I visited every one of Hana's homes, translated her every diary, or found all the descendants of the strangers who helped save her life. It didn't matter how many textbooks I read that told and retold the history of the Holocaust. It didn't matter if facts were incongruent or if anecdotes contradicted themselves. My grandmother's experience—her joy and her sorrow—all intersected in her grief, and that was hers, and hers alone.

CHAPTER 16

LIMITS

I often wonder if one grieves for the departed person, who'll never again experience anything, who'll not see sunrise or sunset, who will not enjoy or have sorrow, who will not have pleasures and disappointment, who will not hear the birds sing or a symphony, who will not enjoy beautiful scenery or paintings in a museum, who will not read a book, discuss a movie, enjoy a play, who will not argue, listen, cook, wash clothes or dishes, serve coffee, chat, enjoy company or solitude. Do we grieve for those who can't do these worldly actions belonging to life, or do we grieve for ourselves that we are left alone, that they left us and we have to fare on our own? Or is it possible that we grieve for both? I almost suspect we grieve for ourselves, us living.

—HANA'S DIARY, 1985

Rabbi Bent Melchior was the only person I remember telling the news about Sergiusz to in person. It was the summer of 2017, and I was once again back in Denmark. I remember feeling nervous as I walked into his apartment. The last time I had seen him was nearly a year before, when I introduced him to Sergiusz. That was just a few days after the wedding party.

As was my habit, I sat down on the blue couch across from him in his red armchair. I squeezed my hands together while I looked at the family tree behind him, guessing that it was now outdated, that there must be too many branches for the frame to hold.

He looked bewildered when I told him that Sergiusz had died. I smiled slightly as I tried to remain calm. "In my professional life, I have had to bury many young people—far too many of them," he said to me as we entered a conversation about Jewish theology in regard to dealing with death. "And you can't really explain to yourself why, and my only answer is that our understanding—our knowledge, our way of thinking—is limited. Mourning has limits. We consider it a known thing that when people have losses of very close relatives, they cannot just go on as if nothing happened. So we actually have rules—rules that are important—so that we can somehow try to recover. That doesn't mean that grief is limited to a certain period, but we have to go back to life in one way or the other."

"Bent, I have never come to a rabbi for answers before. So this is a new experience with Judaism for me." I said, scared of what was about to come out of my mouth. "I don't know how to balance feelings of gratitude now. They feel awful, like a betrayal of reality. When something tragic happens, whether it is my situation with Sergiusz dying, or you and my grandmother fleeing during the Holocaust, we go through this experience and gain this perspective. The world is so much deeper for me now. I see everything differently now. I appreciate what I have differently now. I have more empathy. I think I like me better now than I liked myself before. I feel like I know who I am now. But of course, I wish that it never happened. I wish I didn't know this new me. I don't know how to balance it—to feel like anything good can come from tragedy."

Bent let my confession linger in the air for a minute before speaking. "Well, the funny part about that story is that you didn't come to me to consult a rabbi. I just happened, as a little boy, to be on the same boat as your grandmother. So that brought you to me. You cannot live your life without feelings. You cannot put limits to feelings. Emotions are part of life. You cannot say that these emotions are wrong. We have question marks. And sometimes you are left, as I understand, with a certain confusion. But that is part of the conditions under which we live."

He continued, "I remember when my father passed away—and he

passed away very suddenly, also from a heart attack. But he was much older, of course. He died on a journey, in the central station in Hamburg, in Germany. He was found by the police there. I knew, in the days after that, I had to be strong. If I would somehow collapse, then all would collapse. I should give the speech at the funeral. I should stand by my mother. But when I, a few months later, traveled to America—somewhere I didn't expect it and when I didn't have my defense up—I suddenly broke down and cried. Emotions, at a certain point, have to come out. It is a hefty thing, I think, that it comes out. You will hopefully experience a long life. Many occasions will not be so dramatic as losing your husband, but you will always feel on one side it's tragic and the other side it's happy. It mingles. And we have to somehow keep both things inside."

A few weeks later, on August 8, 2017, I met with Bent again at his apartment in Copenhagen. We had plans to visit the Persson family in Sweden. Bent hadn't seen Per-Arne and his family since the seventieth anniversary of the rescue of the Danish Jews four years earlier.

I linked arms with Bent, holding him steady as we walked to his car—easily the oldest car on the block. He told me it was from 1989 and was in perfectly good shape. "Your car is the same age as I am," I said to him with some concern cushioned in sarcasm. "How are you the former chief rabbi of Denmark and have such a car!"

"This way I can leave the doors unlocked and no one will steal it," he replied with an amused chuckle. "And I don't want the community to think they paid me too much."

I helped him into the driver's side before walking to the passenger's side. "Bent," I said with more concern. "What about the side mirror? It's missing."

"I've been looking at my reflection for eighty-eight years," he retorted, with even more amusement. "I don't need to look at myself anymore."

And with that we were off, ready to retrace history together.

"People are shocked that I still drive," he said to me as he navigated us out of Copenhagen. "I must admit, when I was fifty and I was sitting in a meeting with people who were around ninety, I would run away from the meeting so that they should not offer me a lift."

"So what does that say about me right now?" I responded.

"I think, generally speaking, elderly people will drive more carefully, at least more than young people," he said.

"You just need a side mirror."

"Well, I have one mirror there." He nodded toward the rearview mirror. "So it should be alright."

We went on to have a conversation about old age.

"Of course, you get older, and you have handicaps. I am no longer a candidate for the Olympic Games. But who cares—let somebody else be the candidate for the Olympic Games. But above all, when you age, you lose people. You are losing family. You are losing friends. People pass away around you. When they are my generation, it is nature. But I have an ongoing conversation with the Almighty God when he takes away young people."

"What do you say to him?" I asked.

"I say to him, it doesn't make sense. Here I am, an old man. *That* I can understand. I have lived my life and have had my chances to do something. If I did do something, others have to judge; but I had the *chance* to do something. If I had any talents, I had the chance to use them. Let young people have the same chance. But somehow I don't get an answer. You can say, How can you then still believe that he is there? (Or *she*, or whatever gender you want to give to the Almighty.) Because I somehow accept—or you can say I have no other choice than to accept—that even our ability to think and to understand is limited. Our senses are limited. We can hear—most of us can hear—but only within a certain limit of tones. If they are too high or too deep, the ear doesn't work. You can see up to a certain distance and then no longer. Our senses are limited, so why should our understanding or our knowledge not be limited? Of course it is limited. And even the most clever people say, the more they learn, the more they understand the more they are not knowing. But I hope one day to get the explanation of things I do not understand."

"I came across this quote from the Bible," I said as he drove us through the tunnel to the bridge that would take us to Sweden. "It talks about protecting the widow, the orphan, and the stranger. And I had to stop in my tracks because it spoke so deeply to me and I am kind of new for

Talmudic and biblical literature to really speak to me. But I think about my grandmother as the orphan and the stranger. And I think about myself as the widow. And it feels so personal. In a very uncomfortable way. In an 'it shouldn't be so personal' type of way."

"Don't worry about taking it personal," he responded. "Why shouldn't you take it personal? We talk about human beings for God's sake. We talk about life as it is. With all of its realities, with all of its joy and its sadness. With all of its happy occasions and tragedies. And so you have to accept that here comes something that will be with you. And I told you that we have put limits in weeks and months and years on the question of grief. But we are not unrealistic. We know it doesn't disappear. It will remain as part of you. You will miss that person all your life. But this is, shall you say, the condition of being born—that you accept these things."

As we drove onto the Øresund Bridge, the same bridge connecting Denmark and Sweden that Torsten and I had crossed the year before, I began filming a selfie video and shifted the conversation. "I want to note that we are crossing the Baltic Sea right now, and you crossed the Baltic Sea with my grandmother almost seventy-five years ago. That's pretty incredible."

"It's amazing." he said. "I feel you are quite right. I feel the same thing. And I am so glad that you accepted to go with me, because it gives this trip a deeper content."

"Do you think about the boat ride often?"

"Each time I come here—where we go now—of course, I am thinking of it. But I am not only thinking of it *now*. I cannot read in the newspapers about these people that are drowning in the Mediterranean without thinking that had not some miracles happened, that could have been my fate in the Baltic Sea. I feel that we really survived."

We arrived at Per-Arne's home in the early afternoon. It was a cool summer day with a strong shore breeze. As with every visit before, I walked into the house feeling like I was stepping into a museum of my own family history, except now I held Bent's hand. We were all a part of the tangible testimonies of each other's lives.

Bent, Per-Arne, and Per-Arne's wife, Marianne, greeted each other like the lifelong friends they were, jumping right into a conversation that switched between Swedish and Danish with ease. I smiled at every word, even though I understood nothing.

We ate Danish pastries that Bent and I brought from Copenhagen. Annika and Monica were with us. We all laughed a lot as the language barrier and translations kept the conversation light. The clocks on the wall timed our visit, and as I always did, I documented our visit. I set up a camera on a tripod in the corner and left it there. I also wanted to be in the shot.

"A place is not holy by itself," Bent said to me on the drive home. "It's a question of the people who are there that make a place a holy place. The wood and the cement, or whatever the walls are made of, is not holy, but it is the actions by human beings that can change a place from a normal house into a holy place. And I think that is the kind of feeling I have to enter this little house."

"I want to turn their house into a museum," I said.

Bent encouraged my thought. "I mean nobody else in the world would ever come to Beddingestrand," he stated as his eyes moved from the road to look at me in the passenger's seat. "It was just a coincidence. And it is thanks to little Per-Arne who was just six years old at the time, playing there in the sand and going inside to his father and telling him there was a boat out there. He really did a good deed without knowing he did a good deed. And to stand there at that shore and realize that had it not been, had we not at that time reached this place, we would have ended at the bottom of the sea."

A few weeks after our visit to Sweden, I returned to Copenhagen to spend Rosh Hashanah with Bent. I gripped the banister of the balcony where I sat in the Great Synagogue, surrounded by the rest of the women who had gathered for the evening services. A line Hana wrote in her diary during the war sat in my head like the start of a redemption prayer recounting the past. "Rosh Hashanah takes place amidst all this . . . Gestapo invade synagogues . . . in cars that are waiting outside the synagogues." I overlooked the entire sanctuary, down onto the aged wooden pews and out to the bimah.

The Torah, which the community would restart reading once again, was full of the same stories I had learned as a child in my synagogue in Boston. I could see Bent, his kippah peaked out from his pew, his back hunched. He looked small, sitting in the same seat he always did since retiring from the pulpit. I wondered to myself if the tallit he wrapped himself in was the same one his father once wore. His wrinkled hands turned the delicate pages of the prayer book as he followed his grandson, who now stood as the rabbi at the head of the community. It felt like some kind of miracle to watch Rabbi Jair Melchior, the great-grandson of Marcus Melchior, lead the service. He wasn't much older than I was.

I smoothed down my black skirt, bought recently so I would have something modest for services. I had painted my fingernails black except for my ring fingers, which were a sparkly gray. It was a habit I formed after Sergiusz died. I liked marking something different in a beautiful way. I tried to calm my fidgeting hands by placing them on my prayer book, which was closed in my lap. Where my wedding ring once lived was now a bandage that hid the tattoo I got a week before while visiting Sergiusz's parents in Poznań—a small letter *S*, to commemorate the day I became Sergiusz's widow longer than his wife.

The congregation stood. I followed. I watched as Jair kissed one of his sons on the forehead and wondered if one day I would ever have children of my own.

After services was dinner. Bent invited me to sit next to him at the head table. It felt like I was his granddaughter; he introduced me to everyone who said hello. And after dinner I walked him home. We moved slowly, talking the whole way. He was asking me about the stories I had started collecting from other young widows.

"You have a responsibility to live for both of you," he said to me, bringing up Sergiusz.

"I know," I said, nodding. "I'm trying."

"You are doing great," he told me. "You are creating something with what you feel. In the war, six million died, and there should have been six million more, but I lived. There were many times in my life I should have died, but I am still here. I'm also trying to use my grief for good."

I nodded again as Bent gave a wave to a passerby he knew. Our arms were linked, and I held tightly onto his hand.

"Now, I want to say something more personal," he said, pausing in front of Torvehallerne, a big food market. It was late now, and a few groups of friends sat drinking beer at the public picnic tables.

"Please," I responded.

"That is to say that you have a duty to get married again and to produce children. To make your grandmother's survival meaningful. You are the answer to the evildoers, to the anti-Semites—that you are here. But it shouldn't stop with you. I wish you so much happiness."

CHAPTER 17

KNOW THY HISTORY
AND LOVE THY NEIGHBOR

I am so self-contained. I am a world of my own, a world full of light and shadows, a world full of sorrow and joy.

—HANA'S DIARY, 1940

The one-year anniversary of Sergiusz's death came on September 29, 2017. A group of us went up to Maine to spread his ashes. Close friends flew in from Canada, Mexico, and across the United States, and Sergiusz's parents came from Poland. We stood by Knights Pond together, in the same spot where I was married and where I once spent countless hours with my grandmother as a child. We all wore graphic tees, many of them his shirts, to honor him. I wore the bright yellow T-shirt he was wearing when we met, the one with the clown puking the rainbow.

In that second year without Sergiusz, I mostly stayed still in Boston. I stopped moving around so much and chose to spend the winter months in my parents' basement, becoming something of a permanent house guest. I snuggled with my dog every night and wrote each day. I purged my past onto hundreds of pages and revised the words I had written before, fearing that because grief is so bewilderingly unique and ever changing, I might never be able to tell my grandmother's story.

"It might sound trite," my grandmother once stated. "But I believe what my father said: 'What you have in your head, nobody can take away from you.'" I leaned into this and continued filling my head with memories of the dead. I had conversations with them. I debated with them. I wrote to them. I looked at thousands of my photographs and hours upon hours of video, watching a version of myself from before. It told a different story now. In many videos, I shushed Sergiusz so I could preserve the quiet of my surroundings, not knowing he would become such a fixture in the narrative. I became acutely aware of how I intentionally curated the content of the present to fit the story of yesterday.

I became more social that year and practiced letting my heart open up again. I returned to Israel twice that spring of 2018; the first time was with Sergiusz's parents who asked me to join them on vacation. They wanted to revisit a place he loved. I dated a bit and spent the warm days with close friends. I danced alone in my room whenever I finished a piece of writing, shaking off the loneliness of my grandmother's story and my own. I began wearing lipstick more often, went trail running, and spent time sitting on the porch with my dad.

Some days, I had the urge to take down photographs of Sergiusz and the sentimental objects of our old life in order to make room for the new. In the physical and in the abstract, I practiced making space. Grief still lived in every room I walked into, but many other stories began to fill them as well. I started to feel anxious about what the future would bring as I broke away from my commitment to the past.

In late August 2018, I began packing once again for Europe. It had been just shy of a year since I had been on the farm, which marked the longest time I had been away from my ancestral continent since I began retracing my grandmother's story nearly five years prior. I would stay for six weeks or so, following up on the story I was working on with young refugees in Sweden and speaking at various events to commemorate the seventy-fifth anniversary of the rescue of the Danish Jews. I would visit Sergiusz's parents and spend time with the people my grandmother's story had brought me close to. I would stay on Sine's farm, which had become my routine. I had plans to see Dáša's family—Michael, Ruben, and Miriam. I would visit the Persson family in Sweden and spend Rosh Hashanah in Copenhagen with Bent again. We had decided it would be our yearly tradition.

A week before my flight, I received a message from Annika, who told me that her father, Per-Arne, had passed away. "He died at home," she wrote. "Together with us, and we held his hand. It was still and peaceful."

I sent my condolences, feeling the sharp pain of knowing that in the coming years there would be many people from my grandmother's story I would have to say goodbye to. It was inevitable that the generation of Holocaust survivors, rescuers, bystanders, perpetrators, and witnesses would soon be gone. She told me that the funeral would be held on September 10. I told her I would be there.

September 10, 2018, was Rosh Hashanah and I knew that meant that Bent would not be able to attend the funeral. But we spent the night before together as planned. Jewish holidays are celebrated sundown to sundown, so on the eve of September 9, I again joined the Melchior family in welcoming a new year. The synagogue was now under construction, so services were held in a modest community room. A divider separated the men from the women. I didn't open the prayer book or try to follow along, although many of the prayers I could recite by memory. For most of the service, I just closed my eyes and let the room fade to black as the sounds of us descendants narrated the history of our ancestors.

Judaism had become my international constant. Whether I was in someone's apartment, an aging simple synagogue, or beneath the most impressive ceiling, the call to prayer sounded the same. Sometimes it was the rhythmic sounds of repetitive chants, and other times it was the familiar tunes of songs I learned as a kid. The sounds of Judaism marked life and death. And today I was alive.

Like the year before, I sat next to Bent at dinner and listened to Jair—Bent's grandson, the rabbi—as he gave a short sermon before serving the main meal. He warned us not to let our demons overwhelm the goodness in our life. He gave examples of the mundane, commenting on the ongoing construction in the sanctuary, and of the political, noting the challenges around integrating new immigrants into Danish society. He spoke of the emotional and the historical and encouraged us, saying that in the new year, we should practice appreciation.

"Look at us," he said. "It is simply a miracle that we are here when, seventy-five years ago to the day, we were told to flee because someone else didn't think we belonged. And now we sit together celebrating the new year." He paused. The silence echoed. "And if you have questions of that time, I am sure you can ask my grandfather for stories."

The next morning I left for Sweden. Like habit, my body knew where to go. I navigated my way across the Øresund Bridge, thinking less about seventy-five years before and more about the previous year, when I drove over with Bent. I smiled to myself thinking about how, when Bent and I crossed the border into Sweden, he pulled over to hand me a piece of paper with directions written in Danish. Neither of us had a cell phone with data to use for GPS.

"Bent," I exclaimed. "These directions are in Danish. We are in Sweden. I speak English."

He wasn't concerned. "We didn't have a map in 1943. We'll be fine."

Per-Arne's funeral was held in an old, modest church not far from the coast.

When I arrived, I hugged Annika and Monica and embraced Mari-anne, feeling extra closeness to her as a fellow widow. "I am so sorry," I whispered into her ear, scared at the weight of my words even though they were said in a language she did not speak. My cheek rubbed up against her face, which felt wet from her tears. "I am here for me, and I am here for Bent," I told her.

I followed the Persson women into the church, cameras in hand. They had asked me to take pictures during the funeral. I was given a small program that held the prayers of the service and which was decorated with a photograph of Per-Arne staring out at the Baltic Sea. His birthday and death day were printed on it: October 9, 1937–August 24, 2018.

I took a seat in the row behind the family and waited quietly for the service to begin. Annika's husband handed me a rose and told me it was for the end of the service, when each person would be invited to place a rose on Per-Arne's casket. I carefully kept it next to me. The pews squeaked. Every slight movement made a sound that echoed against the walls. I looked at the casket—it was simple and white, surrounded by candles and flowers. On top there was a cross made of earth and a large bouquet of red roses. They were in dedication to Per-Arne from Mari-anne, who sat just in front of me. They had been together for fifty-two years. I watched as she touched the face of her youngest granddaughter, who sat sobbing on her mother's lap. It was the first funeral I had attended since Sergiusz had died.

Slowly, guests entered the church, about twenty in total. Marianne looked down at her watch. It was a delicate piece of gold jewelry given to her by Per-Arne and made me think of the dozens of clocks that lined the walls of their home. They were a couple who loved time, freezing so much of it for the rest of us.

And then the church bells began to ring. The organist started to play. I watched as the young granddaughter reached for her grandmother's hand and listened as the melody of a dignified death began.

———————

After the funeral, the extended family gathered at Annika's house for coffee and sweets. I sat around the table listening to stories of Per-Arne told in Swedish. I laughed when others laughed and smiled when they smiled, not understanding a word. A family member I hadn't met yet approached me, noting my camera. She told me that her name was Marianne as well and that her father wanted to meet me.

Her father, a man in his nineties named Erik, took my hand and, in Swedish, introduced himself as Per-Arne's brother. Marianne translated. "You are the journalist, right?" he said. "The one who is interested in the rescue?"

"Yes," I replied, my eyes wide. "I have heard about you for years, but was told you didn't want to talk about it."

"Come visit me," he insisted.

I promised I would.

I traveled back to Denmark that evening, again crossing the Øresund Bridge, then a couple of weeks later, I made the return trip to Sweden. Erik had been sixteen at the time of the rescue, ten years older than Per-Arne. I don't know if he decided to revisit his memories of that day in 1943 because his brother, the keeper of the family story, had passed away or if perhaps he had always wanted to talk and I just never asked.

Four of us sat around the table—Erik, Marianne, me, and my translator (an Afghani named Hewad, who was near my age). We ate a big lunch and drank lots of coffee. From the kitchen we looked out a big window to the coast, where we could see the Øresund Bridge. Erik brought me every photo album he had. They were filled with beautiful portraits with handwritten dates from all the way back to the 1920s. When I asked about that day—October 9, 1943—he told me that he had helped his father bring the refugees to shore and that he remembered how scared they were and that one of them had a gun in case they found themselves caught by Nazis. He told me he didn't like to think about it, that it was a scary memory. I then asked if he remembered my grandmother, showing him a picture—the same picture that I had shown Per-Arne. He said he wasn't sure, as it was so long ago, but remembered all the girls from the boat being beautiful. "They looked so different from the Swedish girls," he said, glancing down at the photograph then back to me. "I know I must have had a crush on her."

CHAPTER 18

BORROWED TIME

When I was in Boston and played with Rachael . . . why did I get a twinge of sadness? Why do I so often have this feeling when I'm with my children? It's because I see and feel and know that I have all this behind me, that these times will never come again, that I'm just an onlooker, that I live their pleasures and sorrows vicariously.

—HANA'S DIARY, 1990

In 1996 my grandmother decided to write her own eulogy to be read when the time came. She had been at a funeral at which she was sorely unhappy by how impersonal the rabbi's words were. With her eulogy, she included these instructions:

Upon my death, I would like to donate my organs and eyes if needed. My coffin must be plain pine. Women as well as men must participate in putting dirt on my coffin and must be counted in the minyan. When saying Kaddish, I would like you to think of my parents, Josef Dub, Emilie Dubová, and my brother, Petr Dub . . . Also my aunts, uncles and cousins and grandparents, for whom no Kaddish had ever been said, no eulogy delivered, and no grave had been dug. Due to my parents' foresight and courage, I did enjoy the gift of life. You can add how you perceived me. These are basically guidelines.

The eulogy itself, which I found tucked within the hundreds of pages of her writings, was dated January 1996 and reads as follows:

We all live on borrowed time.

Our lives are temporary, and most of us try to do our best.

Our best to our parents, our siblings, our spouses, our children and grandchildren, our friends, and our community. Some of us succeed for the most part. We do have the strength and the optimism to hope, to go on, to be productive, to be concerned, to love, to discipline, to rejoice, and to support.

We are putting our hopes in our children and the future generations.

They will have the same struggles, agonies, and pleasures we had. However, they cannot learn it through us. They have to experience all of the emotions, from exhilarating to mournful ones, on their own. All we can do is instill in the new generation a moral fiber, sense of justice, loyalty, love for learning, awe of nature, respect for each other, [and the capacity to] enjoy life's pleasures and cope with setbacks.

All this we give through love and example.

I always told my children, when they reached the age of reason, "I give you roots and wings." I hope I have accomplished that. I would like to be remembered as being fair to all my children and their spouses. I was always there when needed and was fortunate, very fortunate in that they, too, were with me when I needed them. I derived great pleasure being a mother, raising my family, without having had a role model. I raised them without loving grandparents, or a family full of cousins, aunts, and uncles, as the Holocaust took care of that. But my childhood was sunny and warm, and I hope I gave the same feeling and security to Nina, Janet, and Peter.

I would like to be remembered for my fairness, love, hard work, and sense of humor.

My grandchildren—Elana, Yoel, Ross, Rachael, Daniel, Emily, and Jesse—should remember that I was fun to be with, that I loved to play with them, both quiet games and roughhousing, and later, to expose them to the finer things in life, such as theater, ballet, and concerts.

Neither with my children or grandchildren [have] I ever panicked, and [I] took life in stride, whatever it dished out to me.

Judaism was an important part of my life, not in spite of or because of the Holocaust. I spoke to children and adults in schools, synagogues, and organizations, never accepting an honorarium. I never carried my loss or tragedy on my sleeves and, except that my children didn't have grandparents and extended family, our home was no different than others.

I was active in the synagogue, B'nai B'rith, League of Women Voters, enjoyed Great Books discussion groups, loved to read, and [loved] good music. I loved physical activities, such as skiing, swimming, tennis, and mainly hiking. I traveled a lot, both to Europe and the Far East, and hiked in most national parks in the United States and Canada. I have been blessed with many good friends—some still from my childhood, many from here. I have also been blessed (so far) with excellent health, lots of energy, curiosity, stamina, and stick-to-itiveness. I loved music, opera, [and] live theater and enjoyed taking my children and grandchildren to these activities.

As a professional, I was a good and respected teacher. I taught French and German, GED, and later, English as a second language. I had compassion and understanding for the new refugees and immigrants. I knew from my own experience what it means to be new to a country, not knowing either the language or the culture. The first time I experienced this was when I fled to Denmark as a fourteen-year-old (that saved my life, thanks to the foresight of my parents), then to Sweden on a fishing boat (my story has been published in two books). Finally to the United States, where I had to start all over again, not knowing the language or the customs of the land.

There was no one to teach me English, show me the ropes, or stretch out a helping hand.

On the whole, reviewing my life, it was a successful one.

Life is a lottery.

I never bought a lottery ticket. As far as I am concerned, I won
the biggest and most important ticket: LIFE—CHAIM. I hope it was
worth it and made it a good and loving one for all concerned.

Mutti

(Hanna Seckel-Drucker)

Hana included an addendum to her eulogy—an abbreviated timeline
of her life. It is everything I have told you in this book but summarized in
a single, simple paragraph, the last line of which reads, "I did it my way."

It's been almost a decade since my grandmother died, and at least
another year will pass before this book is published. I don't know who
else I will grieve for in the coming years, and it scares me that the only
certainty that lies ahead is loss. Every day I think about Sergiusz's young
death and my grandmother's long life. I think about how they were both
twenty-seven-year-old immigrants when they were married in America. I
think about how different their lives were before that. My grandmother
had it so hard, and Sergiusz had it relatively easy—and yet, his death
was the tragic one.

In the fall of 2019, I went back to Europe. It was a short trip, only ten
days. As tradition now called for, I was to spend the Jewish New Year with
Bent. It would be our third year in a row, and this time my mom would
join me. On this particular year, Rosh Hashanah fell on September 29,
and for the first time in a long time, the Jewish calendar matched up to the
Western one the same way it had in 1943, the year of the rescue. It was on
September 29, 1943, that Bent's father told the Jews to flee Denmark. And
it was on September 29 five years before that, in 1938, that the Munich
Agreement—the false promise that Hitler would not occupy all of Czechoslovakia if he were given control of the Sudetenland—had been signed.
That was "the beginning of the end" and where my retracing of Hana's life
had begun. Then, many decades and two generations of survivors later,
it was on September 29, 2014, that I flew to Poland for the first time to
start what I thought would be one year—only a year—of following my

grandmother's story. September 29 meant nothing to me, though, until two years later when Sergiusz died.

When I told Bent I would be bringing my mother along for this year's Rosh Hashanah visit, he was eager and excited to meet her, but not as much as she was to meet him. She had developed the same feeling of urgency to meet Bent as she had when Knud-Arne first wrote to her and she learned that Jensine was still alive.

A week or so before our trip, I opened up Facebook to see a post from Bent's granddaughter-in-law, the rabbi's wife. She wrote that Lilian, Bent's beloved wife of sixty-seven years had passed away. I sent my condolences and asked about the *shiva*, the traditional period of mourning when loved ones gather to share stories of the deceased and comfort the immediate family. It is Jewish custom for it to be held for a week. The granddaughter-in-law told me the dates, and I told her I would be there.

My mom and I flew into Denmark on September 24. The morning of the flight, I hung Sergiusz's wedding ring around my neck. I didn't wear it often anymore, mostly just on anniversaries. Somehow in the three years since he died his ring went from being a marker of loss to a symbol that made me feel like a superhero of sorts. We got off the plane in the early afternoon and did a quick outfit change in the airport bathroom, applied a bit of makeup, and took our luggage to be stored at the train station before taking the metro to the apartment of Bent's son, where the shiva was being held. My mom and I would make it just in time for the final night.

On the corner of a Copenhagen street, we walked into an apartment building and followed the sounds of conversation and loving laughter up many flights of stairs and into a room full of mourners. We put our coats and bags into a pile by the door as I caught Bent's eye from across the room. He smiled upon seeing me, as he always did, and gave me a wave. When I hugged him, his eyes welled with tears. I took his hand. A picture of Lilian sat beside him.

"This is my mom," I said to him. "I'm so sorry that this is the circumstance in which I am introducing you."

"Death doesn't care about our plans," he said with gallows humor.

My mom hugged him and took his hand. "I feel like I already know you," she said. "You are so important for my daughter and for our family. I'm so sorry for your loss."

Bent smiled at her and tenderly touched her cheek. "It's so wonderful to finally meet you."

Throughout that afternoon, as we listened to stories of a life well led, I thought back to the shiva we had for Sergiusz. I wasn't even sure we would have one, as he wasn't Jewish. But my grandmother's diaries taught me that mourning is for the living, so I leaned into the tradition for an abridged three nights. It was so strange to be the centerpiece of death, the symbol of someone who was gone. People said the craziest things to me during those nights when guests flooded my parent's small house. They hypothesized about what caused Sergiusz's death, promised me that I would find love again, and told me not to worry because I was still so young. They probed me about what I would do next: Where would I live? Would I go back to Europe? Would I continue with my photography work? I remembered keeping it together—laughing, smiling, comforting other people so they would feel comfortable around me. I remembered breaking down into an exhausting sob when it was all done.

Now, sitting by Bent's side, just a few days away from the third anniversary of Sergiusz's death, I felt okay. Dare I say it, on some days, I even felt good.

Bent never treated my loss of Sergiusz like it was any less or more than any other death. Grief never was a hierarchy for him, and that day, sitting at his wife's shiva, was no different. Bent spoke to me as if I held some wisdom to bestow upon him, for I was the one who knew what it was like to lose a spouse.

"I dated up," he told me about Lilian. "She was much more beautiful than me. And so smart. But that is what a man should do. Find a woman who makes you better."

My mom and I left the shiva just before the evening prayers began. We still had some travel ahead of us as our first few days in Denmark were to be spent with Sine's family on the farm. We hoped to make it to the countryside before dark. Before leaving, I gave Bent a big hug and promised we would see each other soon for Rosh Hashanah.

"I know it doesn't change anything," I said to him, scared of my own platitudes, "but, I really am so sorry. I love you."

"Rachael," he replied. "You know this as well as I do. Life is like a library. We have these people we love, who change our worlds, who love us back. But like with borrowed books, we get to have them for some time, but eventually they have to be returned."

EPILOGUE

Dearest Mutti,

Do you miss me? I miss you terribly. I often imagine us sitting by your pool in our bathing suits. Your body was so beautiful, deep with wrinkles. My skin was smooth and slightly burned. Your spirit was still lively then, although you knew it would not be in your body for much longer. I think we both knew that the passing time before your time passed was something to be acknowledged.

The family is good, but not without our sorrows and trauma. Every day is a new day, and in that I find some solace. Some days are full of joy and have a soundtrack of laughter. Other days are silent, lived only because one has no other choice. But is this not the extent of the human condition? Are light and dark not dependent on each other? Are joy and grief not the impetus to each other's presence?

As always, I'm getting ahead of myself, sharing my reflections before telling the story. It has been over ten years now since we first sat down to talk. I have completely lost myself in your story, creating for myself an experience out of each of your retellings. What started as a simple family history project has become this web of community. When I pull a thread in one part of the world, the story in another place changes. Your memories have become my landmarks, the symbols of my own past.

I wish I could tell you about all the people I've met—about Sine on the farm, and Dáša's children and grandchildren in Copenhagen, and Rabbi Bent Melchior, and the Persson family in Sweden. I wish I could tell you that it is because of your story that Sergiusz and I got together. And it is thanks to your story that I was able to navigate his death.

I think about you all the time—what you went through and how I will never understand. Grief flows in and out of our narratives on her own terms; I don't get to choose when she completely reframes one of our stories. For a while after Sergiusz died, I thought people were scared of me, but now I think that perhaps it was me, that I was scared of people. Either way, every relationship in my life has become different—some have strengthened, and others have fractured. Death, the one promise of our life, distanced me from those I love more than all my years of living abroad.

There are so many questions I wish I could ask you. There are so many stories I wish I could tell you. You often wrote that life was a gift, that in spite of all your pain and all that you lost, you understood that you had the most precious gift in the world. I, too, feel that way sometimes—grief, trauma, and all.

Mutti, remember in 1992 when you wrote me a letter telling me all about the world? I was only three then. Referencing your childhood, you wrote to me, "The world was bad, crazy, and vengeful then. And today, half a century later, it's no better by much. People will always fight for one reason or another and kill each other."

That still holds true and feels more real now than it did many years ago when I first found this letter. World leaders today appear to be fueled by ego, fear, and xenophobia—a harrowing combination if history has taught us anything. They propagate narratives of "us versus them." And they are raping our environment—repealing protections, caring more about profit than purpose. Every day, the twenty-four-hour news cycle speaks of possible nuclear war and of families being separated. There is rampant gun violence here in America, and racial relations are simultaneously making progress and boiling over. To take a line from your letter to me, "Small children are killed and/or separated from their parents for no reason and no fault. They didn't do anything bad."

The Middle East is still fractured. As if on a pendulum, it regularly gets worse before offering the illusion of getting better. The European

Union also feels like it is on the brink of unraveling; the progress you witnessed is breaking down. The recent refugee crisis, which peaked many years ago and remains a dire problem, has resulted in there being more displaced people in the world than when you were a refugee, after World War II.

Because of your story, I have met young people seeking safety in Scandinavia. Like you, they had to flee their homelands without their parents, and like you, they arrived in Denmark and Sweden without knowing the language or the culture. Hopefully, they will meet good people along their way, people who honor their lives and treat the stories they don't know with as much compassion as the stories they do.

The newspapers report of Nazis again. Anti-Semitism is on the rise. I imagine that much of the rhetoric you overheard as your father listened to the radio in 1938 would feel uncomfortably familiar today. I think it will always exist—anti-Semitism. We are a minority, and the hate and fear people have is so deeply rooted in both religion and history that it will likely never go away, even with all the good intentions of others and the protection that Israel offers. I often think back to what you told me of your parents' attitude about Judaism. "Don't make waves," they said. It seems to me that this might still be the safest approach.

Sometimes I worry that I study too much history to be optimistic. But I don't want to make it sound like the world is a hopeless place. I see people coming together and standing their ground. You would be so proud of young people today. I believe they can save the world.

Your story always gives me hope. There is an idea that is found in both the Talmud and the Qur'an: "If you have saved one life, it is as if you have saved the entire world." The people I have met because of you prove that statement true. Out of a loving family, you became just one. And thanks to the unsung heroes of your journey, generations upon generations have been born.

Hope is much more valuable than despair. Despair robs one of purpose, don't you think? It is why I believe we need more stories like yours, ones that highlight the power of the ordinary person. For if we don't see ourselves as having the ability to make change in this world, what reason do we have to get out of bed in the morning?

But of course, I am still scared.

Sergiusz taught me this Polish saying: "Our grandparents were soldiers so our parents could be engineers so we could be artists."

So, Mutti, the question I pose is this: If I am the artist, who comes next?

Sometimes I feel very empowered by what happened in my life, the fact that I became a widow at twenty-seven. In losing everything, I gained so much, and that fact is perhaps the hardest truth for me to live with. I have found myself feeling happy again, and even thankful. I have the freedom to put purpose on a pedestal, and that keeps me engaged in my daily life. I am never bored, although I wish I could be. I stay active, like you did, and spend a lot of time in the woods.

I feel guilty all the time, though. When I laugh, when I smile, when I feel love, it can feel like I am wronging Sergiusz. It is still really hard for me to tell someone that "things are good" or that "things are working out," because to some extent, every part of my life is now a ripple effect of Sergiusz's death.

I understand that I will never understand what emotions existed deep inside you when you thought about your survival. When I think about how dark a place that must have been, I mourn for you.

Sometimes I do question whether I have done the right thing, the fair thing, in learning and sharing so much of what you went through. But I am certain that if you knew where your journey has taken me and about the ever-growing number of students, old and young, with whom I have shared it, you would support me. Although, you probably would have told me I am crazy for spending so many years wrapped up in what you tried to let go of.

Sometimes I imagine what conversations would be like with you today. I would ask you how often you chose to keep your story to yourself for the sake of others. I would ask if it was hard to lie, to pretend that your past was gentle. I try to imagine what you would say to me if you knew just how deeply I had fallen into researching your history. I think you would challenge my interest. You would question me. "You know enough of this story already," you would say. "Why not care about something else?"

Your writings have become like a bible to me. The way you describe your life at the age of fourteen is as poetic as how you write about your life at eighty. Your diaries and letters are the literature of your past, and each tells a slightly different story. I read and reread your stories as if they were fables, modern-day fairy tales that are constantly changing meaning. Every time I open to a familiar page, I read the words in a new way.

I think often about how you had to suppress your memories, even the good ones, in the name of self-preservation. I know you wondered if your mother would have had the same energy you did as an old woman. Was it she who your active lifestyle came from? When you became a mother yourself, you wrote that you cried out to your parents, that your body and your soul wailed for their wasted lives and their miserable deaths. And when you became a grandmother, you wrote about how great of a privilege it was and wished your parents could have known the feeling. There is a nostalgia and a sadness that comes from imagining what never was, to sit in these daydreams of the past.

Sometimes I think daydreams are a fool's game. Are they not just made-up memories? This letter I am writing to you is itself just a daydream as I know you are dead and the dead cannot hear. But I have read the letter you wrote to your own mother after she was long gone, and it makes me believe there is some sense in speaking to those who can no longer listen.

I wonder a lot these days about who my next partner will be and where we will live. And I have big hopes for my career, although I can't quite define what they are. Also, I think I might want children. I sometimes wonder how differently I will understand your story if I have the privilege of becoming a mother and a grandmother.

I will continue this letter another time. I have been writing for so long, and I'm tired now. But I want you to know something that is really important.

Back when we were talking and you neared the end of your story, you said to me, "Rachael, the big difference between your travels and mine is that I had to burn all of my bridges as I moved forward." Mutti, I want you to know that that wasn't true. The bridges weren't burned. They just needed a couple of generations before they could be crossed.

Forever, with all my dedication,
Rachael

ACKNOWLEDGMENTS

In 2009 I was a struggling college student trying to find my way and eager to spend a bit of quality time with my grandmother. Had anyone told me that those storytelling sessions would lead to over ten years of reporting (and likely a never-ending project), I would have said no way. Luckily, I had no idea what I was getting myself into. Following my grandmother's story has been a decade-long blurring of my professional and personal lives. I walked into homes of strangers from faraway countries as a journalist and left as family. I have met hundreds of people whom I can only identify by time and place as I never learned their names. People who I crossed paths with for seemingly insignificant moments stay with me every day. I remember their kindness, their patience, their personalities.

With a deep breath, here we go with an incomplete list of those to thank. I will start with many of the people you have met in this book. I went out to follow Hana's story with a feeling of ownership, as if this were "my" history. The following individuals humbled me, and my history wouldn't have shown itself to me if they hadn't cared. Thank you, Rabbi Bent Melchior, my dear adopted grandfather, for our hours of conversation and for our international adventures. You are the wisest man I know. To the late Per-Arne and Marianne Persson, and to their children, Monica and Annika, and the entire family—thank you for holding this history close and preserving it for the rest of us. And to Erik Persson and his daughter, Marianne—I am so grateful to know you. Thank you to Michael Bergmann and Let for always giving me a home in Copenhagen, and to Ruben and

Miriam—it's so cool that our families have been friends for four generations. Hana and Dáša would love it. Thank you to Knud-Arne for reading that newspaper. You are the reason I met Jensine and the whole Nygaard family, whom I love and thank as well. Thank you Sine and Torsten for taking me in so wholeheartedly over and over again. I hope you know that there is no place I am happier than on your farm. And thank you to Liva, Lauge, and Silje for being my friends.

Thank you to those who donated when I was crowdfunding my 2014–2015 trip. You made this happen. Emily and Jasmine, thank you for being with me in the worst moment of my life (and for the dance parties that have gotten us through some of the darkest days). Erika, thank you for teaching me to love audio and how to make a podcast. You were not only sensitive to the story but sensitive to me. Thank you to my Tree of Trust, to my Dreams Team, to my Hebrew University family, and to my fellow widows. Thank you to the friends who listened to hours of voice-notes (Sarah) and to the ones who outsourced their parenting to me so I could make money along the way (Elizabeth and Joe). Thank you to those who welcomed me into their homes, cooked me food, hosted me for holiday dinners, brought me into their houses of prayer, and told me their family stories. Thank you to those who paid for my beers, gave me a bed to sleep in, edited drafts of essays, and talked through big ideas. Thank you to the friends who came to the wedding and to those who came to the funeral.

To Hana's cousins, Marta and the late Eva—thank you for being as excited to spend time with me in the Czech Republic as I was to spend time with you. Thank you to the former mayor of Kolín, Vít Rakušan, who cared to preserve this history for his town, and to Zita for hosting me in Prague. Thank you to Judita Matyášová for being so helpful in the early years of this research. And to Jan Jensen for writing the article that Knud-Arne read. Thank you to Annika, Ghazi, Hadi, Mahdi, and the entire Noori family for sharing your story. To Julie Lindahl, for our peace project. Thank you to Stephen Smith for your unwavering respect for the stories I tell of the past. Thank you Stephen Gibson for being a constant reminder that some of the best people I will ever meet are strangers on a train.

To my students, young and old—you are simply the best. Your questions keep Hana's story relevant. Thank you to my fellow educators, storytellers, and to the children and grandchildren of survivors for the meaningful conversation. A special thank you to USC Shoah Foundation, Echoes & Reflections, and Facing History and Ourselves, as well as to my photojournalism community for supporting this work at various stages. And to my Jewish communities at home and abroad—you are my constant and my culture. Special thanks to the Temple Sinai community in Brookline, Massachusetts—you have seen me along at every step of the way. You nurtured me as a student, trusted me as a teacher (thank you, Heidi), and loved me as a community member. Also, to the Temple Isaiah community in Lexington, Massachusetts, for giving a home to the Kolín Torah and to Hana's story. Thank you to my literary agent, Joelle Delbourgo, and to Jane Rosenman and Holly Rubino for your valuable editing along the way. Thank you to Blackstone Publishing for believing in this book. Thank you to everyone who has written over the years to tell me how Hana's story has moved you. Writing is lonely, and your words brought me company.

Thank you to my family. Thank you Jesse for being literally the best brother out there. You inspire the heck out of me. To Rebecca—I love you. To my cousins, aunts, and uncles—thank you for letting me become the unofficial family historian. Each of you has your own relationship with Mutti and our history, thank you for listening to mine.

To all of Sergiusz's family—thank you for loving me. To Danuta and Aleksander—you are the greatest gift that Sergiusz ever gave me. *Kocham Was.*

And thank you to my parents, Janet and Dennis, for giving me roots and wings.

I wrote in the epilogue that I like to write to the dead. So I have to thank my hearts and souls: Sergiusz Scheller, my best friend, my lover, my multilingual thinker—you have expanded my mind in life and in death. I feel your love every day, and I hope you feel mine. And to Mutti—I wish you could know how many people love you.

It feels almost physical how I miss writing into my journal and sharing myself, or with a book. Actually, I could not endure writing, because what affects me most deeply, most acutely, I could never express and don't even try to write it down.

—HANA'S DIARY, 1941

DISCUSSION QUESTIONS

The following questions may be used for personal reflection or in book groups and educational settings. These were created by the author with consultation from USC Shoah Foundation - The Institute for Visual History and Education. Secondary-level educators can learn more about testimony-based classroom resources available to support the teaching of this memoir and the We Share the Same Sky *podcast, developed with USC Shoah Foundation and Echoes & Reflections, at www.sharethesamesky .com/educators.*

1.   Rachael's life has been deeply affected by her grandmother's stories and the journey that she took as a result. How have memories in your own family passed from one generation to the next? In what ways have those stories shaped or influenced how you relate to the world and the choices you make?

2.   Rachael believes that sharing the darkness of her grandmother's story, as well as her own experiences with loss, makes the light of humanity in these stories shine brighter. What do you think she means by this? In what ways do you agree or disagree?

3.   Rachael and her grandmother, while under very different circumstances, both developed deep and life-altering relationships across cultures, faiths, geography, and other divides. What is the value of such relationships to expanding our sense of self and our understanding of the world?

4.   Hana writes that it is best not to think about our vulnerability and to "pretend we are wearing a soft tailor-made suit of armor" that cannot be pierced. How do you think traits like this, which helped Hana and other victims of trauma survive their experiences, can also pose a challenge when seeking to rebuild one's life?

5.   Rachael writes about the significance in her life of continuing to speak to those who are no longer here. What do you think she means by this? Have you had this experience in your own life with someone you lost? (Writing prompt: write a letter to someone who has passed away. What do you want to share with them about your life and the world as you perceive it today?)

6.   Rachael shares that Hana was saved by the kindness of strangers. What examples of this kind of altruism and care have you seen in the world today?

7.   In chapter 13, Rachael writes, "Current events felt strange and cyclical, as though a new thread were being spun into the web of family stories I was retelling." What does she mean by this? How, if at all, do you see threads of the past in your present?

8. In chapter 16, what does Rabbi Melchior mean when he says, "We can hear—most of us can hear—but only within a certain limit of tones. If they are too high or too deep, the ear doesn't work. You can see up to a certain distance and then no longer. Our senses are limited, so why should our understanding or our knowledge not be limited?"

9. The theme of home is present for both Hana and Rachael throughout the book. How is the concept of home experienced as both a physical space and an emotional one?

10. In her eulogy, Hana writes that "Life is a lottery. I never bought a lottery ticket. As far as I am concerned, I won the biggest and most important ticket: LIFE." How does Hana's experience as a Holocaust survivor contribute to her appreciation of life? Do you see this thought as one that conflicts with her survivor's guilt?